START-UP TO SCALE-UP

WHAT FUNDERS EXPECT AT EACH STAGE

ABOUT THIS BOOK

Many dream of high growth. Few achieve it. The reality is that it's a harder cycle to complete than entrepreneurs and founders expect. The risks are numerous and intense. The right funders will give you the space and the fuel to perfect your idea and connect with your market. However, they are going to ask you a series of searching questions about how you are actually going to perform. Written as a realistic guide to meeting their expectations, this book gives you a step-by-step guide to what you have to put in place to become fundable and put yourself on the path to scaling up.

ABOUT THE AUTHOR

Kevin R Smith specializes in lining up the money for entrepreneurs and founders as they grow their ventures. Originally a banker, he has acted as an independent mentor and advisor for the last 24 years, helping to join up all the pieces for start-ups and scale-ups, so they can present the best possible version of their story to investors. Kevin is the founding partner of Boom & Partners, a multi-award winning business advisory firm, a mentor at the Nat West Entrepreneur Accelerator and at The Prince's Trust, as well as being a mentor and guest lecturer at Bayes Business School. He is a columnist on *Startups Magazine* and is a regular speaker on funding for growth. For further details, see: www.boomandpartners.co.uk.

START-UP TO SCALE-UP

WHAT FUNDERS EXPECT AT EACH STAGE

KEVIN R SMITH

NOVARO PUBLISHING

Start-up to Scale-up: What funders expect at each stage

Every possible effort has been made to ensure that the information contained in this publication is accurate at the time of going to press. Neither the publisher nor the author can accept responsibility for any errors or omissions, however caused. Nor can any responsibility be accepted for loss or damage as a result of reading this publication.

Published by Novaro Publishing Ltd, Techno Centre, Coventry University Technology Park, Puma Way, Coventry CV1 2TT
e: publish@novaropublishing.com.

ISBN: 978-1-8380674-8-9
E-ISBN: 978-1-8380674-9-6

A CIP record for this book is available from the British Library.

Designed by Chantel Barnett, Clear Design CC Ltd

For further details about our authors and our titles,
see www.novaropublishing.com.

CONTENTS

Appendices

FOREWORD

In my experience, there are two distinct types of entrepreneur. First, there are those who work on the hoof, intuitively learning from experience, being knocked back, getting up, dusting themselves down and going back with better solutions. Second, come those who are far more formulaic and prefer a prescriptive planned approach.

By nature I am in the first category, but mid-career attendance at the London Business School's continuing executive programme proved invaluable in layering an academic framework over my experience to date. It resulted in a pivotal uplift in my development and a flotation (IPO) on the main list of the London Stock Exchange two years later.

Many of us do not, of course, have the time or resource to attend expensive business schools and in any case, even if we do, thereafter we need constant reminders of what we have learned along the way.

Kevin combines hard-won experience working with a large and diverse number of smaller companies, as well as holding influential positions within corporations across the globe. His easy-to-read style brings the full weight of his experience-based advice to bear in a captivating way. This excellent little book will help you to plan the start and scale-up of your business. It is an ideal read at the start of your journey and then to keep by you to dip into, as you reach various stages and plan your onward route to scale.

Paul Daniels
Chair, Involved Investors

PREFACE

Founders and entrepreneurs need to be many things: enthusiastic and energetic, intelligent and inventive, resourceful and resilient, tenacious and talented. Sadly, too many of them are also unrealistic about how to scale their business. Don't get me wrong, I love the enthusiasm and the whole vibe about working with start-ups and early-stage businesses, trying to ensure that they have the best possible chance of success, but sometimes this can be harder than it should be. Having the vision alone is not sufficient – it needs to be implemented properly.

The most common reason why many founders have unrealistic expectations is that they are over-enthusiastic, only seeing the upside and not doing enough research or having enough knowledge to understand all the risks along the way. Add in the pressures of cashflow and time, and it can all too easily not end in the way expected at the outset.

In total, I have spent almost 40 years working in and around a huge cross-section of businesses across four continents from start-ups to global corporates. I have done this whilst working for banks and governments, as well as in business. For the last 25 years, I have been running my own business advisory firm where I am now entirely focused on working with entrepreneurs, founders and directors, helping them grow their business from start-up to scale-up. In addition to my corporate activity, in more recent years I have become an active mentor doing a lot of *pro bono* work for many organizations.

Through this long and varied experience, I have come across many hundreds of truly outstanding entrepreneurs and businesses. Many have great ideas or have started to develop products or services that are new or solve a problem in an inventive way. But they all share the same difficulties of how to start their business or how to scale it in the way that they want.

Typically, early-stage businesses are starved of resources and getting the right knowledge and assistance into a business at the right time, and in the right way, will determine how the business will develop. The resources most often lacking are financial and experience, and between them they lead to another one: time.

This book has been written based on my experiences

of working with many hundreds of companies over many years as a mentor, advisor and as a consultant. It is intended to be a practical but easy-to-read guide to help you to understand what you must do, why you must do it, how it should be done and what funders expect at each stage.

I hope that by reading this book that you, as an entrepreneur, founder or director of a growing business, will understand better how to transform your business from a start-up to a strong business that is ready to scale, and that you as an individual will be better placed to drive your business forward more efficiently as a leader rather than by force of personality alone. In short, your journey from start-up to scale-up will become easier, particularly as you raise funding along the way.

Kevin R Smith

Founder, Boom & Partners

1.

ENTREPRENEURS AND FOUNDERS

Before you start your business, it is worth thinking about what type of person you are and what you are looking for. For many, starting your own business can be about giving yourself freedom but, like all big decisions, it pays to consider all the angles first.

What qualities make an entrepreneur? What traits do we typically see in their characters? Are they born with these or do they develop over time? Can they be learned? Is it nature or nurture? Whatever the answers, it is certainly true that some people take to being an entrepreneur naturally, whilst others would be so far out of their comfort zone that they would never even consider the idea. In more recent times though, many more people are inspired to set up their own business after having lost their job or finding difficulty getting one, so even the most surprising people are becoming successful entrepreneurs. So what are the characteristics that make a difference?

- **Self-belief.** In everyday life, those with self-belief or self-confidence often find life easier to manage, especially when something goes wrong. For entrepreneurs, these qualities matter even more, as they are sure to have many moments of doubt and experience numerous setbacks. It can be all too easy to give up somewhere along the way. A belief in yourself and what you can achieve gives you the power to keep going.

- **Work ethic.** Nobody has ever said that being an entrepreneur is easy or that it does not take dedication. As such, you must be prepared to work hard and put in long hours and expect to have to firefight at the most inconvenient times.

- **Risk.** Each of us has a different tolerance for risk, from sports to investment, and everything else. To be an entrepreneur means that, by definition, you must have a higher risk tolerance level than many others. You will leave the safety and certainty of a job with a regular salary and pension contributions. Or you may decide to follow that path from the outset even though there is no certain income on a regular basis. Many will go much further than that by investing all their savings or even mortgaging their house, risking all that they have. Whichever is true, it does of course tie in with a high level of self-belief.

- **Questioning**. Just because something has always been done in a certain way does not mean that it should always be the case. Entrepreneurs constantly question things around them and look out for improvements. A constant desire to learn is often part of the questioning process.

- **Open minded**. Entrepreneurs spot the gap in the market for their product or service and then do extensive market research and progress the concept to a minimum viable product (MVP). The best ones, however, remain open minded and listen to feedback from those that they trust as to how the idea might be improved in some way. It can be too easy to fall into 'it's my baby' syndrome and not accept any constructive criticism.

Entrepreneurs then have many qualities and character traits that set them apart. They have self-belief, expect to work hard, have a high tolerance for risk, are questioning and have an open mind. They also know how to build teams and work with the best partners. In my experience, entrepreneurs are either born with these traits or they are developed as they are growing up, either as a child or from gaining experience with age. So even if you were not born with entrepreneurial genes, it is possible to gain entrepreneurial traits by surrounding yourself with the right people and having the right approach. The best founders then may have the right genes and upbringing, but also learn from others and from their own experiences, improving as they go along.

The types of personality that decide to establish their own business are typically focused and driven individuals with a clear idea of what they want to achieve. They are ready to put in large amounts of time and effort to achieve these goals, often sacrificing other parts of their life or free time.

This type of personality is similar to that of a sportsperson. The amount of time, effort, focus and dedication required to become a top athlete of any description is immense. For many, it is the area of their life that all else must revolve around. For both business and sport, this is particularly true for the upward ascent and for the time at the top. Perhaps the only difference is that in sports the time at the peak may be shorter than in business.

But the similarities between business and sport do not stop there. To succeed in sport or business needs a web of support and a good team. Just as high performers in sport rely on coaches, trainers, physiotherapists, psychologists, sponsors and all the other wider team members to keep their mind and body in top form, so entrepreneurs need their own support networks. These often include co-founders, mentors and advisors, accounting and legal assistance, investors and more, whose aim collectively is to ensure that the business as a whole is in top form.

So, whether you are a budding gold medalist or the founder of the next unicorn, the next steps appear the same:

- be focused and driven;

- expect to put in a lot of hours to achieve your dream;

- establish a good support team around you as it is not possible to achieve your goals alone;

- make sure that you are well positioned to take advantage of any opportunities (or luck);

- predict future cycles and trends and adapt your focus accordingly.

Having decided to become an entrepreneur and set up your own business, the next logical question is whether you should be a sole founder or a co-founder and share your entrepreneurial journey with another.

As with every other question that you will have as a founder on your long and meandering journey from idea through to proof of concept, and from start-up through to scale-up, the correct answer will depend upon what you as a founder want, together with what your business does and how you wish to go about it. Whilst it's a personal decision, an accepted set of best practices has evolved because they typically yield the best results in the majority of cases.

Some people are more loners than others, some people are more of a control freak or micro manager than others, whilst others are better at delegating or sharing. Some businesses lend themselves to a requirement of more people with diverse talents, whilst others are fine with sole founders. All these elements will determine how you make your decision.

The simple answer to the question is that the more complex the business and the bigger your ambitions, the more likely you are to want at least one co-founder, both to share the responsibilities and to bring in expert and complimentary talent from the first day. The downside of a co-founder is, of course, that you also share the equity from the outset. But the upsides will, in many instances, more than compensate for that singular downside. These include:

- spreading the burden of decision-making;

- spreading the financial risk and access to investment, either by bootstrapping or via friends and family;

- improving company founders' capabilities, experience and expertise;

- the more founders and the more access to sweat equity that a business has, the more likely it is that it will scale more rapidly;

- the greater the number of founders, the less the need for external advisors, assuming that the founders' experience is complimentary to each other

But whilst these benefits may seem attractive, they may still not be right for you as an individual. Do not forget that you can still get a great advisory board in place that can help in many of the same ways as having a co-founder, albeit more at arm's length.

Many of those who join an advisory board will do so for no ongoing payment but a very small equity stake in the business as it helps to tie their efforts to your interests and provides the expertise required but for no cash outlay. This arrangement will still be much cheaper in equity terms than having co-founders. It will give you higher level and, quite probably, wider support, but it will not be so hands-on as having co-founders.

Lastly, it is of course possible to simply hire in the senior management and day-to-day support that you need to run the business. This option is the best way to preserve your equity, but the flip side is that it will increase cash burn and potentially reduce the runway of your early-stage business. It is only businesses that have either sufficient sales revenue or sufficient funds raised by equity or other sources that can afford this alternative.

The right answer to the question about sole or co-founders can only ever be answered by you. Whilst it may depend upon how you came up with the business idea in the first place, it is much more likely to reflect your personality and your approach to life.

One final note. If there are co-founders then it is imperative to ensure that any intellectual property is owned by the business and not by any individuals, and that there are clear, written, signed agreements in place that cover one or more of the founders leaving or splitting the business. Whilst nobody ever wants to think of the possibility of co-founders falling out with each other, it is a foolish founder that leaves the ramifications of such a fall-out to trust.

2.

YOUR BUSINESS IDEA AND VISION

In order to establish your own business, it is, of course, necessary to identify a gap in the market and have a vision for how you can create a product or a service that offers something unique. It may be revolutionary or simply evolutionary, nevertheless, it has to solve a problem in a new way. It might be an age-old challenge or an opportunity that has been brought about by innovative technology or changed circumstances.

But your vision is the starting point for your entrepreneurial journey and the urge to found or co-found a business. After that initial vision, you can start to refine your ideas and consider what value and size you hope your business might reach one day.

After identifying a potential gap in the market and developing your ideas for an initial product or service, you will next start qualifying them to see if they are viable. Different people and personality types will approach this task in different ways, as indeed they will depending on whether they are a sole founder or a co-founder. Whatever the case, there are a number of essential steps to take from the outset.

Ideation is the creative process of generating new ideas which can be accomplished through a variety of different techniques, including brainstorming with friends or colleagues, and prototyping. If done correctly, ideation is what helps founders and business owners identify the right problem to solve and how best to solve it. These techniques can either be used to source the initial idea or to refine one.

The next step will be proof of concept where the ideas that you have developed are then validated to see how feasible it is to turn those ideas into a realistic business proposition. It involves investigating suppliers and supply chains, manufacturers, coders and developers, costs, sales price, gross and net profits, and everything else required to determine whether the idea can form the basis of a commercially viable business. Your goal will be to develop what is known as a minimum viable product or MVP. Proof of concept also needs to establish if customers will buy what you intend to sell and at the price that you intend to sell it at. The ultimate proof of concept is starting to achieve sales.

As a smaller business, there is an inherent advantage over larger businesses. Your decision-making is often much quicker. The different layers of management often present in larger companies often eliminate any more radical ideas.

All of these details will start to reveal themselves as you go through the various steps of research before writing a business plan and summarized pitch deck. But integral to your vision has to be the question, 'what are you as a founder wanting to get out of it?'.

When anyone is considering doing anything important and potentially life changing in their lives it always pays to think hard, do as much research and gather as much information as you can, and also to speak to as many people as possible. It is often then a good idea to draw up a simple balance sheet of all the pluses down one side of the paper and all the minuses down the other. It will help you consider things from every angle, letting you see what the risks are and what the benefits might be.

At start-up networking events, you will often overhear conversations about the best size to which to grow a business. Different people want different things and have different expectations. Some are looking purely for a business built around their family and other lifestyle choices. Whilst others are really plotting world domination and look to scale as soon as they can.

Perhaps the best insight into these expectations comes from the review of female entrepreneurship that Alison Rose, chief executive of Nat West, conducted for the UK government in 2019. Whilst the main focus of the report was female founders and women in business, it also looked in depth at issues surrounding scaling a business.

Statistically, 11.2 percent of men aged between the ages of 18 and 64 establish some form of business whilst this figure is only 5.6 percent for women. So much for starting a business but what about the question of how big should the business grow to? The same research showed that only 2.4 percent of men grew a business that scaled up to have a turnover of more than £1 million whilst this number was only 0.5 percent of women. There are many reasons why women are so far behind for both starting a business and scaling it; many of them it seems are owing to the extra difficulties faced by female founders in raising investment finance. Thankfully much effort is now being put into redressing that issue.

Crucially, what the research showed was that not everyone wants to grow a massive business and many more operate in sectors where it is difficult to scale a business to any significant size. We must also not forget that many do not have the direct skills or the people around them to scale properly even if they wanted to.

Potentially, the rewards for scaling a business are much greater, but it is more difficult as you have to get all the right elements in place as soon as possible, namely: a great product or service that offers something different; good co-founders and/or senior staff; great sales and marketing initiatives; good systems and procedures; an experienced advisory board; good customer service; well-reasoned and costed expansion plans; and so much more.

The question, therefore, should not be 'how big should I aim to grow my business?' but a subtly, but fundamentally different question of 'how big do I want to grow my business?'. Whatever your decision, just make sure that you take all the right steps to maximize your chances of success of growing your business how you want it to be.

Remember that a smaller, lifestyle business is primarily aimed at providing an income to fit around your time and other constraints. As such, it is unlikely to have any real capital value as a business should you wish to sell it for any reason. However, a scaled business that can stand alone is of more interest to other potential buyers, so it is building a capital value, as well as providing an income. Many founders decide to scale their business specifically with their exit in mind.

3.

READY FOR THE CHALLENGES

For anyone starting a business, there is that delicious and intoxicating mixture of excitement tinged with fear. That is partly the fear of the unknown, but it is also the fear of failure. Different cultures around the world and different upbringings treat failure in different ways. Many see it as a necessary step to success. We all learn much more from what goes wrong rather than what goes right. We might simply have been lucky with the things that work and we never analyse them in the same way as we do failures.

But whatever we might learn from failing, and whether this puts us in a much better position for any subsequent attempts, does not alter the fact that failing in business can still be costly.

According to the UK Office of National Statistics and

Companies House, there are five clear reasons why start-ups and early-stage businesses usually fail:

- not investigating the market properly;

- failure to produce a full business plan with realistic assumptions;

- not enough funding;

- bad location, online presence and marketing;

- lack of flexibility and not staying ahead of the curve.

These are the official reasons and each category does, of course, cover a wide spectrum but, as ever, it is important to look beneath the simple statistics. Arguably, all five of these reasons for failure can be attributed to lack of knowledge, resources and experience.

But taking these five points in order it is of course fundamental to ensure that you have a product or service that the market wants, that offers something unique, that you can build and deliver at a price that the market will pay, and that will produce both positive cashflow and a profit. Having investigated the market properly, assuring yourself and others that this is the case, then you need to consider the other reasons for failure.

Writing a full business plan is the only definite way

to ensure that you have considered every aspect of your potential business, unearthed many of the possible problems and found solutions to those problems. It will also ensure that you produce financial forecasts and, perhaps even more importantly, that you consider the assumptions behind those projections.

Once the business plan and the forecasts have been completed you will have a much clearer idea of the cashflows of the business, both in and out, as well as the timings and expected growth in revenues and planned expenditure in order to support that growth. All of this will enable you to see if and when you will run out of money, the so-called runway, and if you do run out, when you will need to raise finance in some form and how much will be needed. Remember that funding does not have to mean selling a stake in the business, but for many early-stage businesses wanting to raise substantial amounts that does often become the only viable route. Also remember that experience suggests that it is prudent to allow everything to take twice as long and cost twice as much as you might hope. Raising equity will typically take around six months but, sadly, too many founders leave it too late.

Whatever else you get right or wrong in your business, without sales it will not last very long. And sales of course come down to location, online presence and marketing. The exact mix, like everything else, varies from one company to the next, depending on their product or service and the sector in which they operate. Sales do not necessarily mean profit, but no sales definitely mean losses.

Lastly, however good your business is now, and however far ahead of the competition you might be, if you and your businesses do not remain flexible and innovative, staying ahead of the curve, then you will be overtaken by others. Put simply, it is like an aeroplane. If it does not keep moving forward, it will drop out of the sky.

So, they are the official top five reasons why businesses fail, but my answer as to why businesses fail is simpler and all encompassing: lack of knowledge, resources and experience. The good news is that all of these can quite easily be assimilated by working with the right team and partners. So do not be afraid of failure, embrace the excitement, and make sure that you fill the gaps in knowledge and experience that will ensure your business grows and prospers.

Having started to understand the top five reasons that companies fail, you can move on and consider how to turn your ideas into reality and how to ensure that your business is one of those that not only survives but scales successfully.

According to the UK Office for National Statistics, 213,285 businesses failed in the UK in the first half of 2020, a 14 percent increase on the same period in the previous year. Without looking much more deeply into the numbers it is not possible to say for certain how many of those that failed were due to the pandemic and subsequent lockdown, but we would not be far wrong to say that the 14 percent increase, or 26,193 businesses failures, was as a result of the pandemic.

Whilst hopefully the worst of the damage to businesses is behind us, there is no doubt that many are still struggling from wounds inflicted by the pandemic and will fail as the economy recovers. However, we must also remember that many businesses have achieved remarkable success by adapting and pivoting quickly, taking advantage of new opportunities, or indeed just being in the right place at the right time.

Every entrepreneur and business owner wants their business to grow and prosper, not to wither and die, but sometimes it can be too easy to blame failure, or at least the lack of success, totally on outside influences, rather than accepting responsibility for not having taken the right actions at the right times.

It is worth repeating those actions that can help business owners avoid some of the more obvious pitfalls:

- **Understand your market**. It is not only when launching a business that you need to fully understand your customers and market. Constant research and customer feedback are necessary to ensure that your products and services stay relevant and offer the right solution at the right price point. Remember to constantly check what existing and potential competitors are doing.

- **Stay ahead of the curve**. Using the constant research that you conduct, make sure that you stay ahead of the curve and your competitors, and anticipate what the market will want. If you lag the market, often by the time you have caught up, it will have moved on again, thus leading to a permanent and damaging state of playing catch up.

- **Correct business model**. Make sure that the business model that you base your business on is the best one for your business. It should be flexible and you should not be afraid to adapt it over time.

- **Flexibility**. Just as constant market research and customer feedback ensures your offerings are as good as they can be, so constant reappraisal of your business model ensures that it remains relevant. Flexibility in all things is key. Many of the businesses that have done the best over the past few years were those that were not afraid to adapt and pivot their entire business substantially.

- **Communicate effectively**. Communication is far from

being only advertising and marketing. It should be about engaging with existing and future customers, and indeed all other stakeholders. Shout about the good things and the new things that you are doing and don't be afraid to talk about the difficult times in need.

- **Work with the right partners**. Of course, any co-founders and staff members are crucial, but so too are external partners: forming a good advisory board can make all the difference between success and failure; and working with the right project partners can control costs and improve efficiency.

- **Grow sales and grow profits**. Ultimately, surviving in business is about making sales and growing profitability, but do not forget the importance of cash and cashflow, which can be particularly challenging when growing a business. By adopting the first six points here, it will help lead to this last one.

As is evident to all, starting and scaling a business in recent years has often proved to be much more of a challenge than in most years, but by establishing and growing your business in the right way, taking note of all the points above, you will greatly improve the chances of surviving in business.

4.

GETTING HELP

Starting a new business can be a daunting task. Whether you are fresh into business or coming out of a long career but working for others, the challenges that go with being an entrepreneur can seem almost insurmountable at times. What scares you most might be financial, technical, regulatory or any of the hundreds of other areas that need to be considered, but these will vary from person to person and business to business. But three things are certain: the vast majority of obstacles are actually surmountable; help is out there in many different forms; and the joy of succeeding will make you instantly forget all the pain that you have gone through to get there.

One of the most structured ways of getting help is to get involved with one of the many business incubator or entrepreneur accelerator schemes around the country. Whilst any business in its early years can be called a start-up, there are subtle differences: an incubator is designed to help hatch a business from an idea into a start-up so is focused on early-stage businesses, whereas an accelerator is designed to help an existing early-stage business to accelerate its growth to the next level.

The structure of the services offered, and on what terms, can vary considerably. So make sure that you know exactly what you are getting and if there are any costs. The largest fully funded scheme is run by NatWest bank and this is totally free to those being accepted. Other schemes run by other operators vary from being totally free all the way through to charging fees to join and/or taking a minority stake in the business in exchange for a place. As a founder, you may of course decide that any costs involved are a worthwhile investment depending on the benefits offered.

Services can vary from providing free offices, phone, printers and all the other things that young companies need but so often cannot access properly. In addition, they may offer access to help and advice from a wide range of sources. Each of these schemes will have some full-time staff to run the hubs, provide advice and support all the businesses in many ways, as well as organizing and running events to provide training and learning to the participants, although the level of services inevitably varies from one provider to another. As well as the full-time staff, most rely on external mentors who give their time, experience and contacts to the participants. The vast majority of such mentors are successful businesspeople who either run their own companies or who have partly retired and like the idea of passing on their accumulated experience and knowledge. The benefit to the mentors is that they get to see a whole flow of dynamic entrepreneurs and young businesses. They can give them a sense of the realistic, add a steadying hand to their dreams and, who knows, just maybe help them to succeed.

Each scheme will have a varied selection of mentors with diverse backgrounds from finance to sales, from fintech to design, from engineering to gaming, from legal to marketing, from ecommerce to fashion, and virtually any other discipline. Some schemes are focused on specific sectors or disciplines, so the range of mentor skills is more concentrated.

There is no doubt as to the benefit of these programmes as they provide invaluable insight, guidance, knowledge, and contacts to those attending. Indeed, many companies have attended multiple different accelerators in order to gain different perspectives. Data about early-stage business gathered by accelerators consistently shows that those that have been through such programmes are more likely to survive than those that haven't.

Mentors and other sources of help exist outside formal incubator and accelerator programmes but take time to consider the actual role that a mentor could play, how best to choose one and then how best to maximize that relationship. Remember that whilst mentors have accumulated a lot of experience over many years, they have typically become a mentor because they want to help others to succeed. I have yet to meet a mentor with a big ego or one that is interested in playing the great 'I am'. Indeed, most are much more likely to talk about where they have failed and why, as that is often a better learning experience to share with others than only speaking about easy success.

As the entrepreneur, you should of course know in which area you will most benefit. It will be driven by your product or service, how advanced your business is, whether you are considering raising funding and many other factors. You may then decide that your ideal mentor will have a strong background in marketing, ecommerce, fashion, retail, finance, sales, fintech or any other field. Remember that each of these mentors will also each bring with them a lot of wider experience over and above their main focus.

Once you have found a mentor with the right technical abilities, make sure that you like and get on with them personally. You must feel comfortable that they really do understand you, your hopes and dreams, as well as your fears. Some entrepreneurs meet with their mentor on a regular basis; others find it necessary only to contact them at specific moments. Either way, your personal relationship matters.

Just in the process of the mentor asking questions, challenging assumptions and making suggestions, you as the entrepreneur will often gain further clarity on a whole range of issues. Maybe the mentor will simply echo what you had already thought or been told by others. Or maybe, and in my experience this is often the case, they will also come up with totally new points. On occasion these new insights might even mean you totally rethinking your business model.

It is not only experience that mentors bring, but also access to their direct and indirect personal contacts and these in themselves can potentially transform the fortunes of a start-up. Networking takes a lot of time and then turning those you meet into proper contacts takes yet more time. Often real business relationships take years to form properly. So to be given warm introductions to your mentor's filtered and trusted contacts can save a lot of time and literally pay dividends.

If you want access to this type of help, knowledge and advice in a more permanent and ongoing form then this is the role played by members of your advisory board.

They can offer all the help and benefits that mentors do, but are closer to the founders and directors, and play a more proactive role in the business, although not in the day-to-day management. Of all the types of help available, appointing a few experienced and knowledgeable people to an advisory board provides more than many other steps and is also normally a cost-effective way of accessing such advisors.

When thinking of getting help and working with a mentor or an advisory board, think of a twist on the old saying, 'it's not what you know, but who you know'. Instead, 'get to know what they know'. Start-ups are challenging enough. Don't fall into the trap of thinking that there is no help out there and you have to do everything yourself. Or be too proud to look outside. When you find help and make the most of it, you can overcome your challenges and drive your business forward.

5.

YOUR BUSINESS
SHAPE

The shape of your business can be crucial, but the fundamental question is 'how can it be profitable?'. Its actual structure is simply a vehicle that is used to give you as many advantages as possible, whilst at the same time protecting you from as many risks as possible. This should not be forgotten when deciding your business shape.

Often, when a founder has had that lightbulb moment and has decided to set up their own business to develop their idea, one of the earlier questions that they will ask themselves is what legal entity is best for them. Whilst technically there are quite a number of possible alternatives, including a CIC (community interest company) and an LLP (limited liability partnership), for most founders the real choice is between becoming a sole trader or a limited company. And unless it is to remain a small lifestyle business, then the only sensible alternative in most circumstances is to trade as a normal limited company: that is a company whose liability is limited by the value of the shares. The company has its own legal identity and all its financial and other affairs are ringfenced from the founders and any other stakeholders. This structure is certainly the best way forward for most businesses.

Having decided to set up a limited company what are the next steps that are required to mould your new business into shape?

- **Set up a limited company.** The benefits of this are that it is a separate legal entity, which ensures that your personal assets are protected should the worst happen. It is also much easier to ringfence its activities from your personal ones, so it is easier to do the accounts and all other aspects of running your business.

- **Choose a company name.** As well as choosing a company name that you like the sound of and you feel reflects what your new business will do, think how easy it is to remember and spell. Check with Companies House or other agencies that the name is available and that you can also secure the domain name.

- **Use an online agency**. Setting up a limited company in the United Kingdom is extremely easy. It takes about 15 minutes online with a credit card and is cheap. Simply choose one of many agencies and complete the forms. Accountants and lawyers will typically charge several hundred pounds for this as well as the costs incurred, but it is so easy to do, it is normally best to do it yourself.

- **Use an alternative registered office**. By law, every company must have a registered office for Companies House's records and it is where any official documentation is sent. But it can be any address and does not need to be the operating address or the founder's home address. Use the agent's address or that of your accountant or lawyer, as that way your home address is not made public, and it also has the benefit of making the business look much more serious. Indeed, having a city-centre, professional-sounding address can be better in many ways than if it is something like Rose Cottage, Acacia Avenue.

- **Use an alternative address for the director(s)**. Just like a registered office, each director must have an address shown, but you can use that of the agent or wherever else the registered address of the business is, so protecting your privacy when the company details are viewed at Companies House.

- **Filing at Companies House**. Always make sure that everything is always filed at Companies House in plenty of time. Either the agency you used to establish the company or your accountant can do this for a reasonable price. Any late filing will be fined and ultimately the company can be struck off the register.

- **Domain name**. As well as securing the domain name that you will use for your new business, also consider securing other similar domain names. That is, if you will use dot com then also secure dot net or a near variation on the spelling of your domain name. This normally costs virtually nothing but ensures that others cannot get the domains later and cause potential confusion.

- **Trade mark**. Consider registering your company name or logo as a trade mark. It is not necessary to register but depending on the business it can be advisable. This is normally quick and easy to do but can be quite expensive. Consider doing this in the UK (£170) or across Europe (€850). The initial cost is relatively low, but every variant must be registered in every sector that you want protection, so it can be expensive in total as the costs are per individual sector. Many new businesses start by registering in just a core sector. Make sure that applications are direct with government in the United

Kingdom or at the European Union Intellectual Property Office (EUIPO), not through an agent who should not be necessary at this stage. For more complicated cases, it might be advisable to use an IP lawyer.

Having gone through those initial steps, it is time to turn attention to that most fundamental question of how is your business going to make money? It is common that entrepreneurs and founders are generally overconfident. About everything. That goes from establishing the actual business, gaining clients in the first place and through the valuation of the business to how quick and easy it will be to raise funding.

Many founders seem to feel that just because they believe that their new product or service is great then people will want it and will pay for it. This can then lead to the founder believing that they do not need to actually do any research for proof of concept and market validation or to get it to the stage of a minimal viable product.

Decisions about the final business shape and what it is you are selling often rely on focus groups and all the other tried and tested methods of research prior to product launch. Without doing such research, it can be hard to answer the following questions:

- What problem does it solve?

- What is the competition?

- What are the barriers to entry?

- What are your products' unique selling points and why is it better than any alternatives?

- Who will you sell it to and how?

- What will the price be and what profit will you make on each product?

- What are the fixed and variable costs to get your product to market?

- How much investment will it take and how long will it be before your first sale?

- How long will it be until you break even and start to earn real net profits?

- Will you need to recruit staff and when? and at what cost?

These are just some of the more obvious questions. Even with some simple desk-based research, it is possible to start answering them. According to UK government statistics, the biggest reason that companies fail in the UK is that they failed to investigate the market properly. Even major companies sometimes make errors with a new product that fails causing them considerable embarrassment. But for an early-stage business with just one product or closely linked products, failure to research the market is much more likely to result in failure of the company rather than just embarrassment.

In my experience, most founders find that everything will take at least two times as long to achieve and cost twice as much as expected even when the underlying market has been well researched. But the better the research, the better prepared you will be for all eventualities and the better structured your business and approach will be.

To be an entrepreneur needs high levels of confidence and even higher levels of tenacity. But it is important that this is tempered with a sense of realism and being open to listening to advice and even constructive criticism. The old cliché 'fail to prepare or prepare to fail' rings true here.

So many founders claim that their product is unique when in reality any number of much bigger, well-established competitors offer an almost identical product or service, often on a more competitive basis. Confidence should not mean blind faith, but rather it should mean an honesty to conduct in-depth market research so that your business structure and your product can be tailored to make sure that it truly does solve a problem in a unique way, and that you will be able to grow a successful business. Should the research reveal too many difficult truths about your product or the market, then that same confidence should mean that you can make the sensible decision to drop that product and build your new business around something else before it is too expensive and too late. Those that are confident, bold and do solid market research are more likely to be successful.

6.

BUSINESS PLANS

Whether you are just starting up your new venture or are looking to scale an existing one, then having a business plan gives you structure and direction. The value of researching it and writing it is that it forces you to analyse all the areas that will have a bearing on your business and your product or service. The process should start with a simplified business model canvas as a brainstorming exercise that helps you categorize your thoughts under separate sections to try and make sure that you have pulled together all of the areas that need to go into the business plan and then grouped them together sensibly.

The business model canvas itself can be as simple as a large whiteboard divided into areas such as:

- Value proposition

- Customers

- Partners

- Activities

- Delivery channels

- Resources

- Costs

- Revenue streams

As thoughts occur, they can be written on the board or even on sticky notes and placed in the correct sections. This initial review and the draft you start for your business plan are essential first steps to informing yourself about every aspect of your new business and the competition that it will face. It will force you to consider points that you might otherwise have missed.

Once you have spent some time on this scoping exercise, you can start to write a full version of your business plan. It does not need to be excessively long or in-depth, but should go into sufficient detail to cover all aspects of the business. It is essential that it covers areas such as:

- **Your product or service**: what differentiates it and you as a company? what are you doing differently and what factors will ensure that your company succeeds?

- **Your potential marketplace**: how much of the market do you realistically hope to reach? is it just the UK or do you plan to export? how will you develop it and over what time period?

- **Your competition and barriers to entry**: will you compete with large players and how easy will it be for you to break into the market or indeed for others to break into your market?

- **Your management team**: a previous track record always adds comfort so if you do not have all the experience necessary, how will you cover the gaps? Make sure that you include your advisory board and maybe even list out other service providers.

- **Your financials**: both actuals to date and future forecast (with detailed assumptions based on research). These must be realistic and demonstrably achievable. If they are too optimistic, then they will undermine the whole business plan in the eyes of others and also set you wrong targets.

- **Your operation**: what is your process for manufacture, distribution, supply chain and route to market? Describe it so the reader can put the financials and everything else into perspective.

- **Your marketing and sales strategy**: explain how you will market and sell your product or service and how you plan to grow sales over time. Again, this will help add credibility to the assumptions used in your financial projections.

- **Contact details**: make sure you include full contact details and links to any other resources, such as your website.

Do not worry if your plan brings out some areas of difficulty as this is to be expected. What is important is that it demonstrates that you know that these areas exist and that you have thought about them and found solutions.

There should be an executive summary of one or two pages at the front that pulls out all the main points from your plan. Be warned, many readers, especially investors, will only look at the full plan if you have grabbed their attention sufficiently in the executive summary.

Once the initial plan is written it can be beneficial to discuss it with your advisory board or other trusted advisors, as it is likely that they will point out areas that they feel should be included or reinforced. They will probably challenge some of the assumptions made, especially in the financial forecasts. These comments and revisions will put you in a more robust position to defend the assumptions you are making.

Once the business plan has been produced it remains an essential document. It is not something to forget, but should be revised and updated periodically as your business grows and as your needs and aspirations change over time. In itself, it's a powerful exercise in clarifying your thinking, but if you are looking to raise funding by way of debt or equity then it becomes a necessity. As such, updating and refining an existing plan is a much easier task then writing one from the start and, because it is not the first attempt, it should be a better document.

If you are looking to raise equity funding, your company has to have a valuation. The only real way that it can be obtained is by producing a full business plan with financial projections, clear assumptions and future objectives. If raising equity, the management team will be scrutinized for its breath of experience. Any gaps should ideally be filled by the advisory board, which you will show in the plan.

As such, whether it is being done simply as a good management discipline or for more specific purposes such as raising equity, the act of writing and periodically updating a business plan is not only a good idea but should actually be considered to be an essential task.

7.

CUSTOMERS, MARKETS
AND DATA

As a founder, you will find yourself doing a lot of market research about all the areas necessary to validate your idea and to write a comprehensive business plan. All this data on your marketplace and on your potential customers will ensure you have more than a good idea. You are gaining real traction that will can be turned into a viable business. The clearer your understanding of the demographics of your core customer base the easier it will be for you to refine and target your products or services, as well as any future sales and marketing initiatives.

Ideally you want to be able to segment your customers into at least age groups and sex, but the greater detail you can gather the more useful it can be. Concerns over privacy and political correctness can make this complicated at times, but knowing that the majority of your clients are, for example, expectant mothers or young professionals will greatly influence decisions over new products. as well as marketing strategies and spend.

If you can collect this information electronically at the point or time of sale, then this makes both data collection and interpretation much easier. But if your business does not lend itself to that, then it is possible to ask your customers to volunteer that information by way of customer surveys and the like, or even contacting or speaking with them directly.

Examples of data collection and how better to understand who your customers are, together with their shopping habits, are seen from the largest retailers and online stores such as Tesco and Amazon all the way down to local coffee shops. Tesco was one of the first to introduce its Clubcard and this effectively tracks data of what each customer buys, when and from what store, whilst Amazon can even assess what products you have looked at but not bought.

Whilst small businesses are not able to gather data in as much detail it is, nevertheless, fundamental to growth for any business to collect and analyse it. See what similar businesses to your own are doing to gather data and be as imaginative as possible. If you sell online, then this is a prime source of data that can be gathered in many ways.

As well as gathering information electronically or at point

of sale, there are many other tried-and-tested methods. For early-stage businesses, these typically include:

- Establishing focus groups to talk about existing or new products or services, as well as what the focus group would like to see in the future.

- Contacting some of your largest or most frequent customers directly by phone or email to ask some standard questions, such as what they like about your business and what they think that you could do better.

- Emailing your client base a short, anonymous customer satisfaction survey using something like Survey Monkey, keeping it short enough so clients respond.

You are looking to understand your customers in as many ways as you can, such as their demographics, their preferences and their spending habits. Once you have such information you can use it to the benefit of your business in many ways, including:

- **Products**. Knowledge of what your existing customers like about your products or services, and what they dislike, lets you refine what you offer to them. In addition, exactly this same information can be used to guide you in developing new products or services and indeed how you communicate with new and existing customers. If you are also able to obtain information from focus groups and other wider research, you are also then well placed to produce different products, but aimed at similar but different demographic groups, ie, younger or older customers than you have at present. This route can greatly increase your potential market but with only limited development costs.

- **Sales and marketing**. Sales are the lifeblood of any business. Almost every business will market itself or its products in one form or another, whether as a whole or with a focus on specific products. Given that any business, but especially smaller ones, have a limited marketing budget it is necessary to ensure that any marketing spend, for whatever purpose, is as targeted and effective as it can be. The better you know your customer base the easier that will be.

- **Business development**. New products can be developed to target new customer segments and promoted by using the most relevant marketing channel.

- **Customer retention**. Each and every one of us likes to feel appreciated and our opinions to count, rather than just being a number lost amongst the masses. It is much easier for small businesses to accomplish. The process of obtaining and using information brings you closer to your customers. They will feel more engaged with you, leading to higher rates of retention and a better reputation in the marketplace which, in turn, often leads to new customers.

Put simply, the more you know about your customers the better informed each and every one of your decisions will be, and the better placed you are to make sure that your business adequately meets the needs and wants of your existing customers and attracts new customers.

Understanding your customer is not the complete picture though, as once you have this understanding and communication with customers you have, of course, started to accumulate data, which needs to be protected, both from a commercial and from a legal perspective. Two particular challenges stand out:

- **GDPR**. New legislation was introduced in 2018 that makes it a legal requirement for every business that holds client data in any form to register at the ICO (Information Commissioner's Office) and pay an annual fee. Whilst the annual fees for smaller companies are not large, failure to register can lead to a substantial fine.

- **Cybersecurity**. Every business is now online and uses the internet even if it does not sell online. This leaves the business open to cybersecurity threats in many ways. This may be by accessing commercial information or customer databases, hacking emails, installing ransomware, instigating denial of service or many other threats. Any one of these are enough to cause major damage to any size business and can easily make an early-stage business fail. Depending on the business, simple antivirus software on computers may be sufficient, but increasingly the risks have become so large and occurrences so frequent that any business that does not take these risks seriously and does all that it can to mitigate them, whatever the cost, is jeopardizing the whole business.

It can be seen that understanding your consumer and obtaining as much information and data as possible, then handling and protecting that data in the best possible way, has become integral to scaling any business, whatever the size.

8.

FINANCIALS, ASSUMPTIONS AND FORECASTS

A business plan forces you to take a step back. From the knowledge you gain from examining your business and market from many different angles, you can formulate a set of assumptions on which to base your financial forecasts. These will only ever be as good as the quality and accuracy of the underlying assumptions. If the assumptions are too optimistic or wrong in any other way, then so too will be the forecasts.

The most important aspects of the assumptions and the financial forecasts are of course the level of sales, costs, profits and cashflow; and how quickly any of them will grow in relation to each other. From these it then becomes possible to predict how much funding is required and when. What are the points that a funder will expect you to cover?

- **Potential market**. What is the total addressable market (TAM), the serviceable addressable market (SAM) and the serviceable obtainable market (SOM) or market share? The TAM is the total available market for the product or service that you are offering, whilst the SAM is the part of that market that is within your geographic reach. These first two are simple to obtain by doing some market research, although this can be more difficult if your product addresses a new segment of the market in some way. The SOM is what percentage of the SAM do you expect to actually be able to capture. It is here that almost every founder and business plan is much too optimistic. This error then, greatly inflates your sales, income and every other figure, leading to all the assumptions being incorrect.

- **Time**. It is true to say that virtually every aspect of establishing a business and starting to scale can take much longer, and indeed cost more, than might be hoped or allowed for. As such, it is important to expect some delays and any assumptions should allow for this. Otherwise the forecasts will predict everything, from sales to profits to growth, all happening sooner than will actually be the case. This will have a major impact on cashflow, as typically costs will still be running, so the burn rate of the business will be higher for longer, so can then potentially lead to the need to raise a higher level of funding.

- **Costs**. As with time, these are often higher than hoped and any assumptions should allow a contingency, just as they should allow a margin for slippage in time. If costs are forecast to be too low, then the impact on gross and net profit margins, and on cashflow, can again lead to the need to raise a higher level of funding.

- **Scaling**. Any growing business consumes cash, as there is typically a time lag between any expenditure and any income generated by it. That is equally true whether those costs are gentle increases for things such as buying more stock or they are more stepped increases like taking on new staff or getting larger premises. In addition, when scaling it is common to take on more fixed costs, even perhaps converting variable costs like outside contractors to fixed costs by taking on staff. These costs are, by definition, more permanent and can only be undertaken when they can be funded from cashflow or external investment.

If any of the above assumptions are wrong, then they will have an impact on the financial forecasts. In some cases, these errors in the assumptions will lead to relatively minor errors in the forecasts. These differences may be in short-term timing differences, for example, and may not have a major impact on the business. The most common error is assuming things will happen more quickly than they will, whilst the most common large error is expecting to achieve a much higher percentage market share than is realistic. This latter point is the one that is most likely to make the forecasts meaningless and lose all credibility.

Having considered the underlying assumptions, let us now consider the financial forecasts that will be produced from them. The word 'forecasts' means that they are predicted but uncertain. The further into the future they are, the larger the margin for error. Despite the fact that the forecasts are predicting the unknown, there are still a number of aspects to consider in their preparation.

- **Period**. It is generally agreed that forecasts should go out to five years, although it is accepted by all that they are likely to become less accurate the further out they go. In some circumstances investors may want outline forecasts for ten years, although it's rare, and, frankly, rather meaningless unless the business relates to some long-term contracts. Some investors may even be happy with three years.

- **Detail**. Ensure that the level of detail is sufficiently granular for what is required and that they are built up on a detailed month-by-month basis. Do not show a simple linear rise in sales, costs and the like, as it is meaningless. It is necessary to show any seasonal variations or taking on fixed costs for example. Make sure that you know and understand what has gone into the changes.

- **Contingency**. There should always be a contingency built in to allow for sales being lower, time delays, higher costs and all the other unforeseen variables. This would typically be done by being prudent with the figures but can also be done by having a line stating 'contingency' and representing, say, 10 percent of total costs.

- **Sense check**. Once the forecasts have been produced take a look at them: do they make sense? and seem realistic and obtainable? Some founders do not seem to understand that forecasting sales of hundreds of millions of pounds within five years is incredibly unlikely to happen and will instantly deter any funders as it suggests that the founders do not understand the market and the challenges. Again, when sales figures are incredibly high it is often because an unrealistic market share has been assumed.

- **Cautious but interesting**. Whilst it is fundamental to the whole plan to present realistic and achievable forecasts, these must not be so cautious that they do not ultimately demonstrate good growth and healthy profits, as otherwise there is no incentive for an investor to become involved. Such flat forecasts are fine though for a lifestyle business not looking to scale or raise funding.

Just as with all aspects of the business plan, the assumptions and forecasts should be reviewed at regular intervals and updated where necessary, as this is the only way to ensure that the figures remain relevant. It is also necessary that actual sales and other key numbers are compared with forecast, as this will give an early insight into performance and what steps can be taken to improve it.

Any potential investor when doing due diligence into your business will focus on the financial forecasts and the underlying assumptions. They will want to satisfy themselves that the assumptions are realistic and that the forecasts are achievable.

As such, it is always recommended that assumptions are particularly well researched, giving evidence of where market statistics and other such information was obtained, as this starts to build credibility. All assumptions drawn from the underlying research need to be realistic and even cautious, as is the case for more subjective views taken for outcomes such as market share.

Approaching the assumptions in this way will then form a good base for the financial forecasts, which should be approached in exactly the same way; realistic but cautious, as it is always better to outperform forecasts than to underperform them. It is also worth remembering that any serious potential investor will look to evaluate worst-case scenarios, asking what if your sales are delayed, your costs are higher or many other matters that would be detrimental to your business.

These financial forecasts play a major part in arriving at a valuation for an early-stage business, so are essential to attracting funds to scale and in determining how much equity you exchange for that investment.

9.

BUILDING
YOUR MARKET

Having had that initial vision, come up with the product or service that you want to develop and decided that you really do want to become an entrepreneur and a founder, it is time to consider the practical points of your business model and sales channels.

Between your initial idea and this point, you will already have done a lot of research to refine your thoughts, obtain proof of concept and get to a minimum viable product. You will also have at least started writing your business plan and now is the time to consider how your sales will be made.

Be sure that you are covering the fundamentals of your product or market:

- Does your product have special features for which buyers would be prepared to pay extra?

- Is your product aimed at the premium or budget end of the market?

- How unique is your product? does it disrupt the marketplace?

- Who is your competition? small or big? local, domestic or international?

- Where do you sell and what are your ambitions? local, domestic or export?

- How scalable is your business and how quickly can you do it?

- Who are your typical customers? age, socioeconomic group etc?

- Does your product have eco, green, environmental or other aspects that will appeal to certain buyers? If so, be sure to promote them.

- What is your value proposition? that is, why should someone do business with you rather than your competitors?

The initial research is vital. Once you have a good idea of the answers to the questions above, you can then start to turn your attention to the best business model and how your product is best marketed and sold. Put simply, how are you going to monetize your business? As well as the more traditional models of making or buying a product at one price and selling it at a higher price, there are more and more businesses that sell software as a service (SaaS) as a path to high growth. Sales can multiply quickly, when existing clients continue to buy regularly and new ones are constantly joining. Other business models that can lend themselves to growth include franchising and licensing.

Whilst for many businesses, the simple or traditional model of using your own branding and buying something in, adding value along the way, and selling at a higher price and making a margin is the right way to progress, many start-ups fall into the trap of adopting whatever revenue model comes to mind first without really considering the alternatives. Different ways of monetizing your business can make profound differences to its profits and even its chance of success. Running a franchised coffee shop or restaurant might attract many more customers, whilst using a SaaS model and generating recurring revenue is often much more profitable and increases stickiness or customer loyalty.

Having decided on the basic business model that is right for your business, it is then time to focus on how to achieve the most sales from your chosen model and how to make those sales as profitable as possible. You should of course start with the basic tools for any business, such as a strong brand, logo and design, all incorporated into a professional looking website. The domain name will be either the company name or maybe something with an obvious link. The site itself should be clear, easily navigable and load quickly on both computers and smartphones. To gain a high ranking on search engines, design and write your content with SEO (search engine optimization) in mind. Along with your website, make sure that you use social media to the best advantage too.

Depending on your product and your target client, different types of marketing will have the biggest effect and, just as importantly, the biggest return on the cost. These range from the basic and more general steps to the more sophisticated and targeted techniques. An analysis of any marketing spend will give you an understanding of what actually works best for you. Whatever size your business is, most companies should be looking to spend at least 5 percent of turnover on their various marketing campaigns. Some business sectors, such as the fashion industry, spend a much higher percentage.

Here are just some marketing methods an early-stage business might use, as well as a website:

- quality business cards;

- attending or speaking at networking events;

- having a stand at a trade show;

- host events for existing and potential clients;

- using a freemium model (basic part free but with paid for extra content) on your website or app;

- capture as many email and contact details as possible from website visitors so you can do regular newsletters to build loyalty and retain customer engagement;

- quality and eye-catching packaging and signage at point of sale;

- in-house promotions at retail outlets or flash sales online;

- get interviewed by local press or do advertorials (a promotional editorial for a publication);

- advertise in targeted publications;

- targeted email or postal campaign or phone calls with identified individuals;

- partner with another company with complimentary products or referrals;

- customer endorsements;

- consider hosting a podcast or getting invited to take part in one;

- consider setting up a YouTube channel or other online services.

Having set out the building blocks it is important to put all this into context. Have a defined strategy and know exactly what results you are looking for from each type of marketing activity: maybe brand awareness from one campaign and a specific number of new clients from another. That way it is easier to measure what works and what does not. Give each campaign time to work but don't keep pushing an obviously dead campaign, so set a time limit to assess progress.

Make sure that any staff or partners that you work with are aware of any marketing that you are doing as this may provide added leverage. Lastly, be bold and brave. If the campaign fails it will be forgotten about quickly. It is the braver campaigns that have the most impact and are remembered the longest.

10.

INTERNATIONAL SALES

After writing your business plan, identifying your existing and potential market and your target clients, and deciding how best to market and sell your product, you should now of course actually be making sales. But how open has your mind been whilst undergoing this process and how limited are your ambitions? Many smaller businesses, whether early stage or more mature, have a tendency to only look at selling to their home market rather than broadening their horizons and selling internationally.

The population of the United Kingdom is only about 67 million, so why restrict your sales to a market that size when there are some 7.7 billion people globally? Admittedly, whatever your product, the vast majority of the world's population will not be the correct demographic or socioeconomic group to be potential clients, but there is no doubt that selling beyond your home shores will massively increase your potential clients one way or another.

Pre-internet, selling internationally was much more difficult to achieve, more expensive and more time consuming. But in the age of websites and instant international payments, making sales globally is as easy as selling to your home town. The only real difference is the cost of shipping and a little more administration. At this level the buyer would typically pay any import duties or other costs associated with a personal import. As an example of how easy this approach can be, many early-stage businesses start to sell internationally at exactly the same time that they start to sell to the home market. Inevitably one sale in a region can often lead to others.

By starting at this level, any start-up can sell almost anywhere in the world relatively easily and often at no additional cost if the buyer pays for shipping as well as import duties. If seriously targeting a particular market, it is relatively easy and inexpensive to mirror the company's website in one or more additional languages.

One word of warning though, depending upon the exact product or service being sold you should take care to consider any potential legal aspects and product liability issues. Some markets, with the United States in the forefront, can carry exceptional legal and regulatory risks, and many companies avoid the country for that reason alone. However, the US is also a large, affluent market that speaks English so it can also be worth the extra effort and costs involved.

The benefits of trading with the US market are so large that it certainly merits serious investigation, even if the risks demand an open-minded approach. Do not just consider selling directly, but also consider working with some form of local agent or joint venture partner, or possibly selling a licence for the US market to a local company.

Other aspects that should be considered relate to intellectual property rights, such as trade marks and patents. Despite what many think, there is no such thing as a worldwide trade mark or patent, instead the applicant must make many applications in many different markets, which can prove costly, especially with patents. However, to register a single trade mark in a single class throughout the whole of Europe costs a €850 filing fee so that is a good place to start. Even with these countries covered, there are some markets, such as China, where local competitors may disregard the IP and produce locally manufactured, cheaper and often inferior copies. Defending IP can prove to be much more expensive than registering it in the first place.

The traditional way of exporting or opening up an international market was to find a local representative or partner that knew the local market and would act as the person on the ground, dealing with all the import documents and other logistics. It's still a valid form of market entry, but it is, of course, more expensive and so lends itself to larger or better established companies. But for an early-stage business, making sales over the internet is a good way to start selling internationally and find which markets work best, whilst at the same time keeping costs and risks to an absolute minimum. Should one market prove to be a great success then all the more traditional ways of expanding internationally can be used as the company grows.

What product or service your company provides will greatly influence who your target clients are and what international markets best suit you. But whether you provide software as a service, high fashion, consultancy, gin or household goods, there is no doubt that there are many people living outside the UK that also want to buy what your company produces.

So, why restrict your potential market to a population of just 67 million people, or less than 0.9 percent of the global population, when it can be easy and cost effective to reach a much larger audience that will potentially help your business scale much more quickly?

11.

VALUING EARLY-STAGE BUSINESSES

Founders typically establish a business with one of two game plans in mind. Either they want a lifestyle business that fits their work-life balance. Or they want to build a business and grow it with the ultimate goal of building something of value that they can exit when the time is right for them. For any founders seeking to raise finance for their company or to sell it, there will always be the need for a valuation, regardless of whether their priorities are lifestyle or growth.

For larger companies, and certainly publicly traded ones, there are a number of valuation methods that are accepted by all. These would typically be price/earnings ratio or discounted cashflow, but both of these methods require solid data over a number of years and are often better suited to companies with a more easily forecast pattern of growth.

However, for early-stage businesses, valuing a company is much more of an art than a science because the business will not have the long track record to use as a basis. Often, the valuation is based on future expectations rather than present or past trading. These vagaries make the process much more difficult and, it has to be said, the final valuation arrived at will always be more open to interpretation.

There are many different considerations that are used when contemplating the valuation of an early-stage business, but these would typically include:

- Is the company pre-revenue or already making sales?

- Is it still loss making or already profitable?

- What is the size of the total potential market and what is a realistic market share to aim for?

- What are the barriers to entry to prevent new competition challenging you in the future?

- What is the strength and depth of the management team?

- Is there a good advisory board in place?

- How much is being raised and how will the money be spent?

- How quickly is the business forecast to grow?

- Will there be further fundraising rounds?

- Do you already have plans to introduce new products or services?

- Do you have an exit strategy? if so, what is it and when?

Once the above have all been considered, what are the best ways at arriving at a solid and defendable valuation?

- **Comparison**. One way that is often used is by researching similar companies and how much they have been valued at when raising finance or being bought when they were at a similar stage of development. This of course can only ever be an indication, but if it is possible to cross-reference a number of similar companies then this starts to give a good general picture. Remember that valuations vary from one country to the next and that there might also be a specific reason why any particular company was valued more or less.

- **Price/earnings**. This method might still be looked at but will be based on forecast future earnings rather than present earnings as early-stage business that are growing have much higher ratios than those that are more static, as the sales of growing businesses sales are expected to increase greatly in coming years. This makes it much less reliable and so it is not often used. Higher growth businesses and sectors would have higher p/e ratios.

- **Scorecard**. Perhaps the best method to value a company in these circumstances is by using a balanced scorecard. This asks a series of questions related to the business sector and size of the potential market: how experienced are the founder and the team? is there an advisory board? is the company pre-revenue, revenue generating or profitable? what will forecast sales be in, say, five years' time? will the founder be open to training or stepping aside? and many other such questions. Using algorithms, the scorecard then calculates a valuation range. There are a number of such scorecards publicly available and many others available from paid sources.

- **Return on investment**. Venture capital funds and other professional investors look to make a certain minimum level of return on their original investment and use this as the basis for valuing a company, and so how much they will invest and on what terms. This would typically mean that they look at an internal rate of return of between 20 percent and 40 percent year on year, leading to an exit where they make a multiple of ten times their investment. The VC would look to such high returns as many in its portfolio will not achieve them, or indeed might fail altogether, so those that do succeed must pay for other less successful investments.

To complicate matters further, the valuation of your business will typically be higher if you are aiming to raise funds via crowdfunding than if you are in negotiation with a VC. It will probably be different again if you are in negotiations to sell your business. If selling a business, do not expect to get the same p/e ratios as you might see in the financial press as they will be for quoted businesses on a liquid stock exchange and not for private businesses where selling any shareholding is much more difficult. Valuation is a complicated topic and, like everything else, your business is only worth what you can convince someone else it is worth.

Given that valuing early-stage businesses, especially those that are expected to scale quickly, is such an inexact science, it would usually be advisable to use a combination of all of the above valuation methods, undoubtably giving you a range of valuations. Hopefully, the valuations will be similar and, if they are, this then gives a good guide to a realistic valuation. As the founder, it is then important to be prudent and not to try and overvalue the business but to settle on a valuation that can be defended.

If set too high, it will not only jeopardise the fundraising, but it would become damaging to go back for a subsequent round at a lower valuation. As such, it is always better to under-promise and over-deliver and leave some room for flexibility in the future.

12.

YOUR FUNDRAISING CAMPAIGN

After arriving at a well-researched and prudent valuation for your business, you are then able to turn your thoughts properly to the fundraising campaign itself and understanding what is the best way of actually raising funds for your business. The most effective route will vary from business to business depending on: your type of product or service; the size and stage of your business and so whether you are looking for pre-seed, seed, series A or series B funding; what the funds are required for; the size of the fundraising; whether you seek a financial investor, a strategic investor or smart money with contacts that will play an active and informed role; and a whole range of other variables.

But whichever way is finally decided upon, the same

basics will be required, albeit they may vary in the depth of detail required depending upon the size of the raise and the investors that you are approaching. You will certainly need:

- A business plan with a good punchy executive summary.

- A pitch deck.

- A deep knowledge of your business and market with the ability to communicate it.

- A management team with experience appropriate to the size and stage of your business.

- An advisory board that can add high-level support and guidance.

- A valuation that you have reached and the rationale behind it – most founders over-value.

- The amount of equity being offered in exchange for the investment.

- The amount required in the fundraising and a breakdown of how the funds will be used.

Ideally, any written information that a potential investor will require should be gathered together in a central file so that it is quick and easy to access. In addition to the documents stated above, items such as certificate of incorporation, memorandum and articles of association, any meaningful contracts and anything else relevant should be held in the same area. This area is referred to by venture capitalists as a data room and often they will require access to everything in that room. Whereas if raising finance from angels or crowdfunding, it is normal that they would not require all this information, as the level of due diligence is less.

All of this needs to be presented in a professional way. If you are not able to do that, any potential investors will certainly take the view that they cannot trust you with their money or rely on you to run the business well. Even silly mistakes in spelling or grammar can have a detrimental effect on the professional image that you will need to portray in order to raise finance successfully.

Given that there are so many elements to fundraising and that it is an art not an exact science, just like valuing the business itself, means that it will often take longer to achieve than most business owners realise or allow for. That is, it will take longer both from start to finish and day to day. A typical fundraising campaign will take six months from the point at which you start to when you obtain the actual investment funds, although this can, of course, be much quicker or longer. Unless you are a larger business, then you as a founder or as one of a small management team will be diverted for many, many hours every week from actually running and growing your business, which can prove to be detrimental to sales or even the business as a whole.

If a business is looking to raise finance, then it should start its fundraising campaign well in advance and the amount raised should be sufficient to provide a long enough runway to ensure that the business does not need to raise more funding too soon. A runway of between 12 to 18 months is generally considered to be optimum, as if it is any longer then too much of the business is being sold too soon at too low a valuation, but if it is shorter then too much time is wasted on continuously raising finance and not concentrating on driving the business forward.

As such, it can be seen that fundraising is a complicated and inexact science, but the more you as the business owner understand the process and what it entails then the better your chances are of success. You should seek advice and guidance to help you ensure that you raise the right amount of money, at the right valuation, and in the most appropriate way for your business. Some of the fundraising burden can also be shared with someone else, so you can spend some more time on running the business.

13.

ALTERNATIVES
TO EQUITY

Whatever the business, whatever the sector, whatever the stage, the truth is that all businesses need to be funded in one way or another. Until the point that ventures have grown and are generating enough cash to fund themselves, all businesses need access to some form of funding.

But what exactly is the truth about funding? What options are available? What are the benefits and drawbacks of each type? In theory, there is a wide range of different finance options available. In practice for early-stage businesses, many of these may not be available or only in a restricted way. Even so, it is worth founders being aware of them. They may not be available or suitable now, but may well be in future. Knowledge of the possible funding options enables the best decisions to be made.

Most founders tend to think that funding only means equity or possibly grants, but the reality is that there are many different forms of funding, even if some do play a more prevalent role than others. In simple terms, funding can be split into three types: equity, debt and grants. However, a combination of Covid-19 and the entry of challenger banks and other providers to the market in recent years has changed the landscape of what funding is available and from where – and will continue to do so for the foreseeable future.

Whilst accepting that equity funding may be the only realistic way for many early-stage businesses to raise substantial amounts of finance, business owners should be aware of alternative funding options that are available in the marketplace.

Bootstrapping

As a start-up with no track record, it can be almost impossible to obtain funding from any source. In addition, how can any founder expect others to take a financial risk in their business, if they have not been prepared to do so themselves? As such, not only must the founder invest their time and effort for free, but it would also be expected that they have invested hard cash from savings, other income or even mortgaged their house.

The next obvious step is to persuade friends, family and fools to invest into the business. This can be done in every way from informal loans to formal investments at an agreed valuation and with shareholder agreements. At this stage, these investors are investing because of the personal connection and belief in you as a founder, rather than taking a hard, dispassionate, commercial look at the venture, and they will typically do so with virtually no real due diligence. The funds typically come from friends and family, but it is the lack of due diligence or real commercial approach that is the reason that the fools' tag is often also added.

It can also be possible to raise some initial development finance from a non-equity crowdfunding platform, such as Kickstarter or Indiegogo. Individuals support start-up companies by donating funding in exchange for the first products developed or free services or subscription once the company is actually trading. As these funds are neither exchanged for equity nor do they need to be repaid, it can be seen as a form of bootstrapping and funding for the initial steps. This method of funding can also act as a way of getting proof of concept and developing a minimum viable product, as well as starting to market your business and products.

Debt finance

Traditionally, banks and other lenders are seen to be there to provide loans to companies. This debt finance can come in many different forms: overdraft; short-term working capital or stock financing; leasing; invoice discounting; asset finance; term debt; property mortgage; and many more. If accessible, debt can often be quicker to obtain than raising equity, but it is only normally available to longer established companies. Traditional banks typically want three years' worth of trading history and newer lenders either want to see 18 months of trading or will lend based on monthly sales. These criteria do of course mean that it is not available to earlier stage businesses and funding size is normally limited.

One major benefit is that founders do not need to dilute their shareholding by selling part of the company, although there is an immediate impact on cashflow as the interest and principal of any loan facilities are repaid. Equity finance can often be the only viable option for early-stage businesses, as they either require large funds to scale operations or they are viewed as too risky and have too short a track record for the banks and other lenders to consider. Despite what many small business owners might feel, the reality is why should a lender put its capital at risk for a much lower return in the way of interest rates, rather than participating in the upside of the business?

Grants

There are many grants that are available from many different sources within a landscape that is constantly changing. As such, it is not possible to go into specific detail, but it is certainly a form of funding that is worth considering. Exactly what grants are available depends on geographic location, industry, type of product or service, whether you are applying as a sole company or as part of a consortium, and many other variables. The grants themselves can be from just a few thousand pounds through to many hundreds of thousands of pounds, even for early-stage businesses. Some of the bigger and better known grant schemes are from Innovate UK and Horizon 2020. A good example of sector-focused grants is the Arts Council.

Applying for grants can be a time-consuming process, so must be balanced with the chances of success to evaluate if it is worth the management time. However, as well as the obvious financial benefits of winning grant funding, is the fact that it is effectively strong third-party endorsement of your business, and this is something that resonates well with potential investors. Also, as grants are neither equity nor debt, they do, of course, preserve the equity of the business for the existing shareholders and preserve cashflow as neither the principal nor the interest needs to be repaid.

Given that applying for many grants can be a lengthy, detailed process and that experience of what is expected improves your chances of success, you might choose to work with a professional grant writer. Many of these work on a success-fee basis.

One universal grant for which it is easy to apply, has a quick processing time and is available to most companies is the tax credit for research and development. Many more companies conduct qualifying R&D activities than most would believe, not least because the focus of the grant is on innovation rather than invention. Even loss-making companies can make a claim and claims can go back two years. If your company has not looked into R&D tax credits then it really should do. This scheme is covered in more detail in the appendix at the back of the book.

Government schemes

In addition to the more normal government grant and loan schemes, there have been many more introduced during

2019 and 2020 that were intended to ease the financial pain of the pandemic. The biggest and most widely available schemes for businesses were the Coronavirus Business Interruption Loan Scheme and the Bounce Back Loan Scheme but these came to an end in March 2021. However, the Recovery Loan Scheme replaced them in April 2021. It is a subsidized loan that is 80 percent government guaranteed and will lend between £25,000 and £10m to companies of any size. Various funding options are available for up to six years and are available through the majority of major lenders.

As well as loans, some new Restart Grants of up to £6,000 are available in England to non-essential retailers, and up to £18,000 to the hospitality, accommodation, leisure, personal care and gym sectors.

These were exceptional grants and schemes for exceptional times but if accessed when they were available, businesses can still be benefitting from them now.

Convertible loan notes

A convertible loan note is a form of debt that will turn into equity when the next funding round takes place or at a backstop date if a funding round has not been completed before then. The benefit of this form of financing is that it is not necessary to agree a valuation of the business at the time as this will be determined at the valuation of the next fundraising. In exchange for accepting this level of uncertainty, the convertible loan note will typically give investors a discount of 10 percent to 20 percent off the valuation when they are converted, so will benefit from investing earlier.

The conventional structure for a convertible loan note falls outside the requirements for tax breaks for investors (see Appendix 1 about the Seed Enterprise Investment Scheme and the Enterprise Investment Scheme). So it can adopt an ASA (advanced subscription agreement) which is a specific form of convertible loan note that does comply with the tax requirements for SEIS and EIS.

The truth about alternative funding options then might seem complicated. With a little investigation and maybe with some help, the number of options should ensure that at least one is right for you and your business.

14.

THE RIGHT INVESTOR

For those business owners who decide that they wish to obtain investment funding in order to scale their business, the inevitable first question is of course where to start? That question is followed by the supplementary one of 'what are the fundamental differences between the different types of investor that I might get?'.

Taking the plunge and deciding to start your own business can be one of the biggest decisions that many of us will make. Having set out on that course of action it is imperative that we do all within our powers to ensure that the new business is structured in the best way and with sufficient resources. For many it will mean making the decision that to scale properly means the need to raise finance other than bootstrapping.

Raising finance can mean different things to different people depending on the business that they have established, and the size of their dreams and ambitions. The differences can mean anything from does finance mean debt or equity? through to how much will the business need and will it need more in the future? The answer to this question will start to lead you in your decision-making process as to how to choose the best investors for your business.

As already discussed, finance can come in many different forms and all have their own benefits and drawbacks, but equity finance can often be the only viable option for early-stage businesses as they either require large funds in order to scale operations or they are simply viewed as too risky and have too short a track record for the banks and other lenders to consider. Both an upside and a downside of taking equity is that investors tend to be there for the longer term. This is just one reason why choosing the right investors for your business, at the right time, will impact on the future of the business for a long time.

Having decided that raising external equity is the best route for your business, then is the time to really consider exactly what type of investor you are looking for. As so often, the best and most accurate answer will come from the best and most specific question. So what are the primary matters to consider before starting to formulate the question about where is it best to obtain investment? These should be on everyone's list:

- What stage is my business? concept, feasibility, pre-revenue, post-revenue, profitable?

- What stage funding are you looking for? that is, start-up, pre-seed, seed, scale, series A, B or C?

- What type of product or service does my company provide? and who are the customers?

- How much investment am I looking for?

- What percentage of the business am I prepared to sell?

- What is the funding to be used for?

- What length of runway will this give my business?

- Will I need subsequent rounds of funding in the future? if so, then what size and how soon?

- Do I want a financial or strategic investor? and do I want smart money?

- Do I have a good advisory board and am I prepared to allow an investor a seat on the board?

Your answers to the above questions, together with any others that are more specific to your own business, will start to lead you to the best route to investment in your company.

When raising equity, as the size of the investment

sought grows, and the number of previous investment rounds that have been previously undertaken increases, then the terminology changes. Whilst there are no hard and fast rules as to what size constitutes what phrase, they do nevertheless provide a general frame: the smallest and earliest external fundraising is referred to as pre-seed or seed; and then it progresses up through series A, series B, series C and the like. As such, the progression goes hand in hand as the company scales and matures.

In order to do full justice to your own requirements, it is necessary to go through a detailed decision-making process, but some generalized guides can be summarized and are shown in the following tables.

Table 1: size of investment, stage of development, investment round

Small	Medium	Large
Start-up / early	Early	More developed
Seed	Seed / Series A	Series A+
Friends and family	Crowdfunding and angels	Venture capitalists

Table 2: valuation

Lower	↔	Higher
Venture capitalists	High-net-worth individuals and business angels	Crowdfunding

Table 3: levels of involvement, assistance, board seat, control

Lower	↔	↔	Higher
Friends and family	Crowdfunding	High-net-worth individuals and business angels	Venture capitalists

Table 4: interest or ability to participate in future rounds

Less	↔	↔	More
Friends and family	High-net-worth individuals and business angels	Crowdfunding	Venture capitalists

Whilst these tables are simplified, it makes it clear that each type of investor brings different sets of benefits and drawbacks, creating a series of trade-offs.

By way of an example, looking at the above it is apparent that venture capitalists are more likely to be the investor of choice if you are looking to raise larger amounts of funding, probably for a follow-on round for a more developed business and that the VC is best placed and most interested to invest in further rounds. In addition, they are looking to provide an active input to help the business to grow but that means a seat on the board and potentially more interference than other investors. Potentially the biggest downside is that they will often negotiate harder and will want a larger percentage of the business, thus leading to a lower valuation.

Crowdfunding, business angels and high-net-worth individuals are typically between friends and family and VCs on every one of the scales above but in varying orders. Friends and family are always at the bootstrapping end of a company's journey and fundraising activity. Whilst they are quick and easy to deal with, and normally undemanding, they rarely represent smart money and their resources are limited.

The questions above, and the answers to those questions, as well as the simplified guide above, are an indication to what type of investor is typically right for what type of company and at what stage. But that is only part of the story.

The right investor is so much more than just the one that is prepared to pay the highest price for the best valuation, or even the smartest money. The right investor will make all the difference to how well and how quickly the business develops, as well as ultimately how large the business might grow.

Crowdfunding investors are typically the least directly and personally involved. Business angels and VCs are normally more likely to play a direct role. Different types of founders and different types of businesses are best suited to different types of investors. Make no mistake that an investor, especially one that plays a more active role, is a long-term partner. Like every partnership, your choice of partner will have a great impact on you and your business for many years to come. For that reason, it is imperative to find a route to the investor with the same ethos and aims for the business as your own.

15.

BUSINESS ANGELS

Equity funding for businesses can come from many different sources and which is best will depend on many individual factors. Once a founder's own financial resources and other bootstrapping options have been stretched as far as possible, and any alternative finance options have been fully explored, then it is time to investigate pre-seed or seed equity funding.

The most typical ways of raising early-stage equity funding are either from wealthy individuals typically investing tens of thousands of pounds each or from crowdfunding that opens up the investment round much more to the normal retail investor investing anything from £50 upwards. The individuals investing larger amounts are normally referred to as business angels.

A business angel tends to be a wealthy individual or those with sufficient liquidity and risk appetite to be interested in investing meaningful amounts in early-stage businesses, often attracted by the tax breaks for enterprise schemes (see Appendix 1). They are often also referred to as either a self-certified investor or a professional investor. Many such investors are often self-made who have built up and sold their own business and look to re-invest into other businesses, often in the same sector so that they can use their market knowledge or expertise. If an individual already knows the sector or can instantly see the potential of your product or service, then they will often make a quicker decision than if funding is obtained from other sources.

This type of investor is referred to as bringing smart money, as alongside any money that is invested, they are also able to bring sector specific or relevant experience and knowledge, as well as useful contacts. Not all angel investors bring smart money and many are content to invest passively in the right businesses.

Some angels are serial investors whilst others only invest once. Also, some angels prefer to find opportunities and invest individually, whilst others invest via one or more angel networks.

An angel network is typically a group of small serial investors that look to invest directly into early-stage businesses. Often, each individual would invest between £10,000 and £50,000 although it could be much higher, and the network would secure the whole funding round in a syndicate. The network provides the opportunity for a series of companies to make pitches in the style of Dragon's Den to the investors at an event, charging a fee in the region of 7 percent of monies raised, although it can vary considerably depending on the total amount and the level of services. Some networks also charge a presentation fee of a few hundred pounds for being able to make the initial presentation. The benefit of this option is that you are put in front of a range of serious individual investors.

When taking investment from angels, it is imperative that all investors in the same round invest on identical terms: that is, the same share class, price and all other details. It can be all too easy for one or two potential investors, typically those that are looking to invest larger amounts, to try and negotiate better terms such as a non-dilution clause or a better price. Once that is allowed to happen, it is inevitable that other potential investors will find out, then it becomes a race to the bottom with all the investors wanting the more preferential terms.

Sourcing angels via an angel network can guard against the likelihood of having to negotiate on a case-by-case basis as the network will often lead the negotiations and the investors will only be able to invest on the same terms. In addition, when sourcing investment from angels there will always be a need to do multiple presentations. At least if the presentations are to networks, then you access a number of potential investors each time.

One downside of taking on multiple angel investors is that if there are too many individual investors, then the cap table can become messy and cluttered. (Your capitalization table records all your shareholders and how much equity each holds in your company.) Going forward, it can take up significant time to manage, particularly in communicating with one or more significant minority shareholders who might attempt to interfere too much. Having an investor who is not a professional can potentially lead to a lot of wasted time and effort in answering too many questions from a potentially ill-informed large minority shareholder.

To summarize, getting investment from angels, either individually or collectively through networks, can be a good way of funding early-stage businesses. If you are lucky enough to find the right angels, then any investment decision can be made much more quickly compared with venture capital or even crowdfunding. However, if the angels are not found quickly, then it can often be necessary to do numerous presentations, which can take many months. So you might be lucky and find investment quickly, or it might take much, much longer.

16.

CROWDFUNDING

Crowdfunding as a major source of funding for early-stage businesses is relatively new on the funding scene. It has transformed the market as it fills what was a huge gap between friends, family and business angels at pre-seed and seed level, and venture capital for better established companies. In today's market, it is now enabling many businesses to develop and scale to the point where more traditional and larger funding from VCs can then be sought.

There are many crowdfunding platforms to choose from, but the first major one in the United Kingdom, and still the largest, is Crowdcube. The other major UK provider is Seedrs. They have historically led the way in innovations such as nominee shareholding and a secondary market for shareholders. Many of the smaller platforms focus on an industry or a sector, which may suit more niche companies, although the pool of investors is smaller.

It is worth noting that there are also a few platforms, such as Kickstarter, that are specifically aimed at funding ideas, prototypes of products, social campaigns and the like, and these tend to be much smaller campaigns. Also, these raises are effectively advance payments and do not require the fundraising company to part with any equity.

Lastly, there are sites that focus on crowdfunding debt rather than equity, the original and still the largest of which is Funding Circle. However, these typically require the borrowing company to have been trading for some time and are, therefore, not accessible to early-stage businesses.

Most equity crowdfunding platforms operate on broadly the same parameters, albeit there are variations in some of the detail. On the larger platforms where most of the funds are raised, campaigns can be anything from about £100,000 to £5 million, but are more typically between £150,000 and £2 million.

Crowdfunding is best for businesses with products or services that are aimed at consumers (B2C) rather than at other businesses (B2B). It is not a strict rule, but certainly the business and what it produces must be relatively easy to understand by many people without needing specific technical knowledge. But, as ever, it is important to tell the right story in the right way in order to generate interest and understanding and, thereby, a desire to invest.

It is true to say that valuations for businesses on crowdfunding platforms would often be higher than if raising finance from a venture capitalist or even an angel but it is crucial that founders do not over-value the business, as it reduces the chance of a successful raise. In addition, should the business then require further funding in the future, it is best if the valuation is seen to have risen.

The biggest mistake that many founders make when considering raising finance from any source is leaving it too late. As a guideline, it is sensible to expect a timeline of six months from start until obtaining finance from whatever source, although this can of course be shorter.

Crowdfunding campaigns require significant planning and effort prior to launching the campaign. For at least six months before the campaign, you should be maximizing your database of customers and other contacts, so that these can be contacted in the pre-launch campaign and asked to pre-register if they have a potential interest in investing.

Crowdfunding platforms will typically expect a business to be able to demonstrate that they have a soft commitment for approximately 60 percent of the target raise before they will be taken onto the platform. The first step is 'private live' where those that have pre-registered an interest are able to invest first via a link (and possibly take advantage of any entitlement to tax breaks if available), before the campaign is then moved to 'public live' and can be seen on the general platform and invested in by everyone.

The campaign needs to get off to a good start and maintain momentum, as many potential investors, no matter how interested, often do not actually invest until they see many others doing so. In addition, the platforms have funds that automatically invest when certain percentages or other conditions have been met. These additional funds boost the campaign further and encourage yet more investment.

Statistically, some 80 percent of funds that go public live are successful, typically going on to over-fund and raise an average of 140 percent of the target amount, although this can be stopped at any time. The success rate reflects the fact that the platforms reject many applicants and for those that they do accept they ensure that they do not go public until fully ready.

Fees are typically around 6 percent but are only payable if the money is raised. It is important to underline that unless the full targeted amount is raised then no monies are handed over and are indeed returned to the potential investors. The fees cover all aspects of the legal procedures before, during and after the raise, as well as issuing share certificates, any certificates for tax breaks and all other such documentation.

Each investor becomes a potential buyer of your product

or service, as well as an ambassador for the company, and each existing customer or contact is a potential investor, so crowdfunding can be a powerful marketing and brand-building exercise.

Seedrs announced that on Christmas Day 2020 it passed £1 billion invested on its platform since launch, and in 2020 more money was raised for more companies, from more investors, than in 2019. Interestingly, the Covid-19 pandemic and lockdown seem to have made little difference to crowdfunding, with the same levels of retail investment going across the platforms as previously. There are a slightly reduced number of companies raising however, but for those companies still in a position to do so, this can only increase the chances of success.

Clearly the best chance of a successful raise is to ensure that the business is fully prepared and that the founders, directors or someone that is closely involved in the fundraising has a full understanding of the processes, algorithms and all other aspects of crowdfunding.

17.

MAKING YOUR PITCH

It is true to say that most people have heard of a business plan, but fewer, certainly those not involved in early-stage businesses, have heard of a pitch deck. A pitch deck complements the business plan and stands alongside it. Just as the full business plan has an executive summary of one or two pages to catch the readers' imagination and encourage them to read the whole business plan, then the pitch deck can be seen as an alternative form of executive summary.

It is used by a company to introduce itself to potential investors and is normally the first information that they see. As such, this document can often be the difference between taking discussions forward or not, so it must capture all the essentials of your business and make it interesting so that the recipient wants to know more. It can be sent by email or presented live or on a video call but either way it is the door opener. The business plan is a long, detailed document typically produced in Microsoft Word, whilst the pitch deck is normally between 15 to 20 pages in length and often produced in Microsoft PowerPoint. It is also a much more visual document designed entirely to sell the business to potential investors or lenders, or anyone else that reads it. It must grab the reader's attention immediately and encourage them to want to know more.

It is important to use pictures, graphs, tables and the like, to get as much of the important information over as succinctly as possible and to reduce the number of words required. It needs to tell a story and there is of course a real art to this. Think of it as a trailer to a forthcoming blockbuster film and you start to get the right picture.

The information contained should enable the reader to understand the company's product or service, the advantages it has over rivals, the size of the market, how much it is raising for what amount of equity and how the money will be spent. It must therefore include projected financials and a pre-money valuation of the company (that is, the value of the company before any additional funds are raised). It is also best to include a timeline of significant events in the company's history. Also ensure that it provides full contact details and links to any other resources such as your website.

Producing the bones of a pitch deck is relatively easy

once the business plan has been completed. Given that it effectively acts as the elevator pitch of the company and first impressions are crucial, I would suggest that it is one thing that is worth spending time and money on to ensure that it looks the part and includes all the required information.

Both the business plan and the pitch deck can of course be produced fully in-house or handed over to an external specialist who can produce professional documents for a fee. Like everything, that decision will be dependent upon the in-house ability and time available, but do not underestimate how long it will take.

Having produced a good, informative, eye-catching pitch deck, it can then be used in a number of ways. Firstly, it can be sent to potential investors and others that are interested in your business so that they can look through it at their leisure and then you can speak with them and discuss any questions that they may have. If this route is taken it is also the opportunity for you to underline any specific points that you want to draw their attention to.

Alternatively, you can present the deck to them either in a face-to-face meeting or virtually on a video link. This method is arguably much better as it enables you to add more detail and to emphasize any aspects that you consider to be of particular importance to your listeners. These pitches can of course vary in length but would typically be for between five to ten minutes followed by time for questions afterwards.

In order to make the most of the pitching opportunity it is important to remember the following points:

- **Tell your story**. Any potential investor sees many decks and pitches, so make yourself stand out from the rest. Tell your story in an engaging way and grab their attention. Talk around the pitch deck rather than read it out. Make sure that it is an interesting story and told well.

- **Show your personality**. Investors in early-stage businesses invest in the founders as much as they do the business itself. So don't be bland in telling your story and making your pitch. Let your personality and your passion for the business shine through. Remember to smile.

- **Keep focused**. Just as you keep the pitch deck succinct, make any presentation succinct too. Keep your presentation focused and ensure that it follows a logical route, one that flows with ease.

- **Maintain eye contact**. Whether your pitch is live or to camera, maintain eye contact and appear confident. Whatever you do, do not read your presentation, as not only does this mean that you are not looking at your audience, but will always come across as you not really knowing your business, as well as it sounding monotone and boring. Investors will easily be put off.

- **Answering questions**. Whatever the scenario, there will always be some questions following your pitch, so make sure that you are fully prepared and ready with your responses. Make sure that you know your numbers, as this is inevitably a focus for questions. If you do not know the answer, it is better to say something like 'I am sorry, but I do not have that information to hand but will happily send it to you later', rather than stumble or be caught out trying to bluff.

This combination of a slick, concise, professional looking pitch deck, together with a confident and knowledgeable pitch, will transform your chances of obtaining finance. Between them they make the difference between being easily overlooked and moving on to more detailed discussions with potential investors.

So, be concise, focused and confident, both in the deck produced and in your pitch. It often makes all the difference between raising finance or not.

18.

TELL YOUR STORY

Any marketing guru will today press home the importance of telling your story as a business. It might be about why the business was established, the thinking behind the products, the ethos behind all that you do, or even about you as the founder if it is a smaller business. Essentially, all of this is about branding and image but told in a softer and more personal way. So what are the best ways to tell your story and promote your business?

After setting up, there are some logical next steps, irrespective of what your business actually does. You have to start making sales at a profit to re-invest in the future and pay shareholders. In the early days of any business, it is difficult to make a profit as so much time, effort and cost is focused on building the product and brand, as well, of course, as making those all-important sales.

Sales can be generated in any number of ways from word

of mouth through to major advertising campaigns, but one thing that almost every business, large or small, has in common is the need for a website. Google and other search engines are now such an integral part of everyday life that the first action that many potential customers will make is to look at your website. Some of the most fundamental issues to consider to ensure your website is fit for purpose include the following:

- **Image**. Think what image your business will project; that is, serious, fun, professional, quirky, youthful or anything else. Whatever image your business and products will portray should be reflected in your website. Make it look like it is written by the target customer and think hard about what they would want to see.

- **Branding**. In the same way as your image, reflect your branding on your website. Make sure it is clear to see and, for the sake of consistency, it is used across any other promotional or public-facing materials, such as social media.

- **Web builders**. Unless you have a design and marketing background or great computer skills, it is normally best to hire professionals to build the site. Doing it yourself will normally take much valuable time and distract you from the business and will often result in an inferior end product. The website is so important that it is money well spent and there is definitely an element of 'you get what you pay for'. But keep it simple and quick to load as research by Hotjar Analytics suggests that 53 percent of users abandon a site if it has not fully loaded within three seconds.

- **Content management**. Make sure that the website is based on a good content management system, such as Webflow, as it will be much easier to update and to make changes in-house, so reducing ongoing operational costs.

- **Keep it fresh and updated**. Whatever your business does, make sure that the website is constantly refreshed with new content as this helps to keep existing customers engaged and return to the site more frequently.

- **Make it mobile friendly**. With more and more users accessing websites from smartphones or tablets, it is crucial that any site is mobile friendly and easy to use. Indeed, Google has relatively recently changed its algorithms for ranking sites by giving more weight to access from mobile devices.

- **Use analytics**. Understanding who is looking at your website, what is attracting them, how long they are staying, and all the other details that the free analytics tool from search engines like Google can give you.

- **Call to action**. Whatever else your website shows, ensure that it is easy to find contact details and also that there is a call to action. That is, to buy or, at least, to request more information. Remember, the website is, first and foremost, a selling tool.

Using this approach should give you a website that helps to generate leads and sales. Now you can really start to promote your business. If we look around us, we will see numerous different examples of how this is undertaken, from promoting the specific item to be sold at one end of the spectrum, through to general brand or image awareness at the other end. Early-stage businesses generally focus on directly generating sales of specific products or direct messages about what it is that the business does. It is typically only larger household names that start to move over into general brand and image promotion.

Early-stage businesses typically have limited cash resources and need to ensure that they get the 'biggest bang for their buck'. So differentiate between sectors and products, identifying what promotional activities work best in each case.

Whatever routes and actions are chosen, track the return on your investment to better inform future spending and promotional decisions. Social networking can be both relatively cheap and highly targeted, as well as being easy to track, whereas other activities such as posters in buses or on the Underground can be both more expensive and more difficult to track. Many companies often overlook that new customer acquisition is always far more expensive than customer retention, and the best way to retain customers is to ensure good customer service and great, engaging, communication.

Loyal and repeat customers are also the best ambassadors for any business, as they promote your product or service for free to targeted potential and new customers. A personal recommendation from somebody whose opinion that they value is much more likely to turn into a sale than a random promotion, no matter how well targeted.

One maxim from the marketing industry is that good news travels fast, but bad news travels even faster. Preventing bad news is best done by ensuring that you and your business deliver a quality product or service, as well as ensuring that customer engagement is maximized in as personal a way as possible. One of the many changes post-lockdown is that many businesses have learned the importance of more personal engagement with their customers. They have moved much more towards making them feel valued and away from the hard-sales pitch. It has become important to tell your customers how much you care about them rather than just going for the hard product sell. In order for any of the above to be true, any business must know its customers, both existing and potential, and ensure that the right message is delivered in the right way through the right medium to the right audience.

To summarize, the best way to promote your business is to know your customers, know exactly your product or service and at who it is targeted, and to provide top-quality products coupled with top-quality customer service. These strategies should ensure a high level of customer retention whilst also providing the best opportunities for customer acquisition. The bottom line of this strategy is that increased sales lead to increased profitability and a growing business.

We all communicate every day in both our social and our business lives but, let's be honest, some do it better and more effectively than others. The word 'communicate' can be interpreted and applied in many different ways. Those that enjoy communicating often find a style or approach best suited to themselves and this is also often the way with businesses.

But what does this mean from a business perspective? Put simply, communication is at the heart of all that any business does. Not only must it communicate efficiently internally with staff, suppliers and contractors, but also with all the other stakeholders in the business and every other body that it interacts with. Crucially though, it must communicate with existing and potential customers, which is the area open to the widest definitions and interpretations.

Business communication can have many different forms and underlying messages, and these can, and do, change over time, both for the individual business, but also in terms of general best practice. This was best demonstrated during lockdown in the first half of 2020 when marketing communications switched focus from the 'hard sell' to 'we care about our customers and will protect you'. Any business trying to communicate and advertise in the more traditional way was seen as not caring and this caused potential damage to the business.

So, what lessons can any business with intentions of scaling take on board?

- **Empathy.** There is no doubt that post-lockdown all communication, irrespective of who it is with, has changed. Communication, both internally and externally, now displays a softer, more caring side, which has to be genuine. Do the right thing for the right reason and that will still, nevertheless, support your business.

- **Marketing**. As already touched upon, advertising and marketing is still a crucial part of maintaining or growing sales, but be aware of the change of mood of your customers. Whatever the marketing activity or the message that you want to get across, ensure that it reflects the true concerns of your customers and potential customers now, rather than what they were six or twelve months ago.

- **Internally**. During any time of uncertainty, it is lack of information that is often one of the most difficult things to cope with. Fear of bad news is often worse than actually receiving bad news and then being able to move forward. Employees that feel taken for granted or not treated well will rapidly lose motivation and productivity and, once lost, it is hard to recapture. Communicate well and regularly with any staff about anything that might impact them. Trust in your staff and most will repay that trust many times over.

- **Finances**. One mistake that many businesses make is not to keep their bank or other funders informed early enough if they see a potential need for further funding or to renegotiate existing funding. As far as any bank is concerned, no news is always bad news, whereas entering into communication early can often resolve any issues.

- **Contact information**. Over the years there has been an increasing move towards making it more and more difficult for customers to find and access contact information and speak with a person about sales enquiries or complaints. Whilst this is done in order to save costs, I have yet to meet one customer of any business that does not see this as detrimental, and it often leads to loss of sales and an increase in dissatisfied customers. Just as empathy has made a resurgence recently, so has demand for personal service. This is an area where early-stage businesses can truly stand apart from their competition.

Good and clear communication has always been important in any walk of life, and it is no surprise that great orators have often also been the best generals or company leaders, as they have inspired trust and people to follow them. Good and clear communication is now more crucial than ever and getting it right will not only enhance every aspect of your business, but also your bottom line.

19.

BUILD YOUR TEAM

Your team is made up of many components or layers, rather like an onion, in that there is the core management team, the outer management and then the outside advisors. Your ability to grow will depend upon the quality of the team that you recruit to make it all happen. Its composition will vary from one start-up to the next: not just as to who you will need now, how you will find and attract them, and how you will incentivise them, but also as your business scales over time.

A good starting point for finding the right people and adopting the right structure is to ask as a founder: 'what are my own arears of expertise and what areas do I either not know about or am not confident that I know enough about?'. If you are a sole founder then it is likely that you will need more assistance, as often co-founders team up with someone who has skills complimentary to their own.

Once you have identified where you require help, you can then decide whether it is one-off or whether it is more permanent and is going to grow and drive your business. You will then be clearer about the basis on which you are going to work with them. The one-off type of help includes specific services such as accountants and lawyers, whilst the more ongoing type are people who you feel you want by your side as they will make a difference to your business in both the immediate and the longer term future.

One-off or contracted services are there to assist with the closer inner circle, so care needs to be taken to find the right people for the right roles. Often the best way to find them is by personal recommendation or reputation.

Whilst both types of assistance are needed in a business, it is the close inner circle that will make the biggest difference, as they will be able to provide the broadest range of support over the longest period of time. It is for that reason that this inner circle is even more carefully selected because of what added value it brings to the business.

Hiring staff at any level can be time consuming in searching for them and then onboarding them into your business. As an early-stage business with relatively few staff, every recruit has an impact, so getting the correct ability, attitude, and cultural fit has more bearing on the business as a whole.

To make sure that the best solution is found there are a number of rules to follow when hiring staff:

- **Sourcing**. Using an agency to provide pre-qualified candidates is a traditional route but can be expensive due to the fees. As a small business, it can often be better to take on people already known to you or close and trusted associates.

- **Titles**. Be careful what title you give people, as needs change as the business scales. If you call someone chief operating office, chief technology officer or chief marketing officer, it becomes awkward to recruit somebody else over them as the business develops and needs different talent. Remember that your business should be free to grow in every direction as you scale.

- **Incentives**. Many younger businesses can have limited cash resources and getting the best talent into the business might not be affordable if considering just salary. One way around that is to offer shares or share options so employees can benefit if the business does well. However, in any contracts do make sure that there is a 'bad leaver' clause to ensure that any shares are returned should they leave in difficult circumstances.

As well as bringing together as strong an inner team as you can as members of staff, experience suggests that the best performance is best with the support of an advisory board. Ideally, it should be made up of four or five experienced and trusted individuals who have a broad range of experience, filling any gaps among the founders and senior team. Often the majority of the advisory board's members play little active role, but are there when needed, although it is better if one or more is much more active.

So what exactly does an advisory board do and why is it often the best help an early-stage company can get? Ideally the board as a whole is able to bring all of the following benefits between them:

- open access to contacts in the sector;

- provide knowledge and expertise in areas that the founders and management do not have;

- provide guidance;

- guide and question the founders and make sure the business stays on track;

- ensure the founders deliver milestones on time and on budget;

- help the founders develop the business and scale it.

These members of the advisory board are often prepared to work for a small equity stake and fee. The amount varies depending on the added value and the amount of time spent. The two benefits to the founders are that it preserves cashflow and makes sure that the interests of the advisory board are aligned with that of the founders and the business as a whole.

Parting with equity is always a difficult decision for founders and rightly so, as it should be guarded carefully, but the success of your business and achieving scale can often depend upon getting the right help and advice. If the company does not have the cashflow or finances to pay for the best help, then releasing some equity is a viable alternative. After all, a hundred percent of a company that has failed because of the failure to get the right assistance is worth nothing.

Remember, getting the right partner for every situation will often radically change the outcome, because if you get it wrong then the consequences vary from wasting time and money, to hampering the growth of the business and potentially much more. There are of course slightly different rules for finding the best partners depending upon if they are short-term, project-based partners or, much longer term, more integral partners.

When building your team there are some basic

considerations that can be applied almost irrespective of whatever role you are looking to fill.

- **Use recommendations**. Perhaps the easiest is to use personal recommendations and contacts. If someone that you trust and respect makes a recommendation or personal introduction, then it should rightfully carry more weight than a cold name obtained from a random source.

- **Project cost**. For shorter term or project-based partners then cost is perhaps a more relevant benchmark than it is for long-term partners, as long as you feel that the partner is able to deliver the desired service to the level expected in the time required.

- **Added skills**. Using the right partners will not only fill a skills gap but a time gap too. In the majority of cases, external relationships, short or long term, are sought as they plug a skills or knowledge deficiency in-house. What is sometimes not understood though is that as a founder, or partner, in an early-stage business, your focus should always be on growing that business and guiding the business as a whole. As such you will not always have the time to fulfil all the roles for which you are capable.

- **Relationship and shared values**. For shorter term partners, shared values are less relevant than for long-term partners. You do not need to personally know, or indeed like, your accountant or lawyer in order to get the accounts or contract finalized. However, for long-term partners a shared ethos and good cultural fit can be highly relevant, as in order to develop a proper working relationship there should be a much higher level of personal trust and respect.

- **Added value**. With any partner try to look through just the obvious contractual requirements and see what added value they bring. That is, wider expertise or knowledge, good and diversified contacts, and other similar assets that you will then also be able to access. This added value is especially important in longer term relationships and should often be seen as the most important differentiator rather than whatever the direct cost might be.

- **Leverage**. As a young business, you will require skills from experienced, more senior partners, but you simply cannot afford to engage them full time. Working with them externally is an excellent way to achieve this by paying an agreed monthly retainer or a daily or hourly rate for when you need assistance. This gives you all the access required but at greatly reduced costs.

- **Advisory board.** Having an advisory board is recommended for any business as it helps keep the founders or directors accountable, as well as on target and focused, whilst at the same time they are able to offer advice, assistance and contacts. All of this increases the chances of success of the business. It is precisely for these reasons that investors feel much more comfortable and like to see an advisory board in place.

It can clearly be seen that getting the right short-term partner is important, but getting the right long-term partner can, quite literally, help to make or break your business.

20.

BUILD YOUR NETWORK

Networks are a powerful way of telling your story and communicating your brand. Indeed, meeting and knowing the right people can make the whole scaling process much easier.

As the old saying goes, it's not what you know but who you know. It's often said in a disparaging way, as in the 'old school tie' is more useful in life than being clever, working hard, or looking for opportunities to make your own way in life. But if we open our minds a little more, it is apparent that there are many ways that knowing the right people really can help you make those next steps, whatever they may be.

We all understand the phenomenal reach that social networking can have and the multiple different channels that are available. Whether you use Facebook, Twitter, Instagram or any of the other myriad such platforms, all are subtly different. They are great tools for communicating different messages to different audiences. Whether telling your story, strengthening your brand, or indeed promoting specific products or services, social networking can produce great effects, as too can SEO (search engine optimization). For businesses, LinkedIn should also be on this list, as it is the only purely business-focused social networking tool.

However, in many ways virtual networks have nowhere near the power of face-to-face networking. The pandemic and the associated lockdowns have certainly demonstrated that virtual networking has benefits such as being able to reach a wider geographic audience, but most entrepreneurs would agree that face-to-face, human contact beats all else.

However, getting the real power out of networks takes effort, time and imagination. It involves a lot of one-to-one meetings, attending seminars and networking events, working on not only your company's brand but also your personal brand. Asia is almost purely relationship driven and whilst the West is much more transaction driven, nevertheless most people would still prefer to work with someone that they know and like and have met before. That is, someone in your personal network.

We each need to accept that no matter how good we might think we are, not even a genius at the top of their game can be good at all things or have time to do them all. The right partners are best found through our own networks. Personal contacts or introductions always work best as they carry the endorsement of someone you trust. This is immensely powerful in business.

Some of the more obvious benefits that the power of networks can bring include:

- improved marketing and visibility;

- increased sales;

- unexpected opportunities;

- cross-selling and co-operation opportunities;

- joint referrals leading to increased sales or revenue streams;

- better advisors and advisory board members;

- access to complimentary products and services so leading to greater client satisfaction.

The dictionary definition of a network is 'an interconnected group or system' which itself implies that it is an intricate web or matrix and not just a relationship between two points. The power comes from when a number of these points, or contacts, are introduced to each other and all start working together in a win-win situation.

But the real power of networks is in the multiplier effect. Put simply, the more dots that there are on your radar, the more the chances of joining them together around you and growth becoming exponential. Consider the simple sum $2 + 2 = 4$: with networking, it can often equal five or more. A better way to think about it is replacing the plus with a times: $2 \times 2 = 4$. But the more people you have in your network the greater the impact becomes:

- $2 + 2 + 2 = 6$, but $2 \times 2 \times 2 = 8$

- $2 + 2 + 2 + 2 = 8$, but $2 \times 2 \times 2 \times 2 = 16$

- $2 + 2 + 2 + 2 + 2 = 10$, but $2 \times 2 \times 2 \times 2 \times 2 = 32$

Well, you get the idea. The greater the number, the greater the effect. By viewing the effect as a multiplier rather than as an addition, the growth in the power of your network moves from the linear to the exponential.

But caution is also required, don't fall into the numbers trap as so many people seem to in their private lives on Facebook or other social networks. A real network's power is more about the quality of the people in your network rather than the sheer number, although a large network of quality contacts is the perfect goal, of course. Sheer numbers might be useful in some circumstances for promotional type activities, but it is the personal, known and nurtured contacts that are the ones that bring the power and produce the multiplier effect above.

Another important factor is that a network is at its most powerful when it is clearly a two-way relationship and both sides are winning: treat it more as a list of friends that you want to help and they might be able to help you, rather than as a database of contacts just there to be used. Karma can often prove to be beneficial, even if the return is not until many years later.

None of the above is new to any of us. But when you are heads down working in your business, it really can make all the difference to put your head up sometimes and get out there, and make sure that you are working on the bigger picture by building and nurturing a quality network.

It is worth noting that some people are afraid of networking and others love it. But for all the reasons stated above, attending networking events can be some of the most important hours in your working week. They have to be the right events, as it is all too easy to go to a different one every day. The benefits and your enthusiasm will soon start to diminish. Choose the right ones and it can be surprising who you will meet, how useful it will be and how much fun it can be. Of course, some will be more useful than others and there is not always an obvious reason for the difference.

There is absolutely no doubt that knowing the right people can help in business. If you have a good, broad range of contacts then there is of course a much higher chance that you will know someone with the skills or knowledge that you are looking to access at any given time. And if you do not know anybody directly then there is still a good chance that one of your contacts will know someone and can introduce you. A warm introduction is a hundred times more likely to be taken seriously than a cold call.

21.

YOUR OPERATING PLATFORM

Different types of businesses require different operating platforms, from offices to retail space, from factories to warehousing, and more. But what all businesses have in common, whatever their size or sector, is that they need to have systems and procedures in place and somewhere to operate. As any business scales what type of systems it requires to operate efficiently will need to grow and change with it. Typically, the smaller the business the more flexible it can be, which can be advantageous for existing and prospective employees and business partners.

Most businesses are having to change many aspects of their operating platform in order to adapt to the post-pandemic world. For some, such as those in the hospitality sector, life has been more difficult than for others, such as those that are predominantly office based or where sales are primarily online.

For them, remote working is becoming the norm. But it should not mean having to work remotely. Effective communication with colleagues and clients can be more of a challenge, but it is mostly about adapting the operating platform of the business.

Working from home means that employees have more flexibility and removes the cost and need to travel to an office or fixed place of work. Many conscientious staff actually end up working longer hours than when in an office environment. Potentially, it can cause added difficulties with computer systems, data security, internal communications, idea generation and a host of other aspects, but all of these can be overcome by understanding the potential problem and adapting your operating procedures to mitigate them.

Over recent years there has been much research into preferences of office workers by the likes of Gartner, Deloitte and PwC. All suggest that the vast majority of office workers would prefer to work in the office for two or three days a week and from home for two or three days a week. This flexibility gives a better work/life balance for those polled.

In one specific survey conducted by CBRE, only 6 percent of respondents replied that they wanted to return to the office full time and only another 10 percent wanted to return for the majority of the week. Compared to this total of 16 percent, almost 28 percent stated that they had seen the full benefits of working from home and wished to stay working fully remotely. But the biggest conclusion from the survey is that 57 percent of people wanted to work a minimum of two days per week, every week, from home or, at least, not in the office.

Employers that do not recognise this shift in expectations run the risk of failing to attract the staff that they want, as well as having premises and other resources that are not matched to the requirements of their workforce.

Businesses are looking for much more flexible lease terms for offices and retail space as more people are working from home and shopping online than ever before which has led to an over-supply of certain types of premises.

But whatever the business, and wherever it operates, systems and procedures are the foundation for scaling in any meaningful way. Some company structures are inevitably simpler than others and, of course, the complexity of the business will dictate what is required.

However, the reality of life for the majority of small start-ups is that they are established with almost no systems or procedures in place, as they are often so small that the founders do all the jobs themselves or, at least, oversee them. Even many start-ups that are more than just the founders have no real procedures in place other than the rudimentary ones regarding job descriptions for founders and any staff. Sadly, so many of these start-ups just never get round to the next steps.

A recently established small business or a one-person operation can get away with operating in that fashion as there are typically not many people involved and not too many moving parts to keep an eye on. But as a business grows in size, then inevitably so does its complexity, as it takes on more staff and the number of moving parts to try to co-ordinate growth. What was once possible, becomes less and less so, and steps need to be taken, not only to ensure that the business is able to operate efficiently at the present point in its growth, but also so that it will be well placed for future growth.

But what every business owner will learn sooner or later, is that what works in a small start-up simply does not work as the business starts to scale. It is typical for start-ups to be continually firefighting and doing many things in no particular order, other than that they have become urgent. Not only is this vastly inefficient, but this system of working means that the founder or directors never get to follow a well thought-out plan, and the business itself will suffer accordingly. All of this leads to the need to set up proper systems and procedures for how the business operates.

Initially, it takes time to set up such procedures. Once in place, they not only save considerable time whenever an action is taken, but they also guard against errors and the need to constantly firefight, thus saving money. The more that any procedure can be automated the better, as long as this does not impact negatively in any way on the customer journey or experience.

Examples of simple systems and procedures that should be used by all businesses would include, but certainly not limited to:

- Have proper founder and employee contracts in place, as well as standard procedures when hiring new staff. Ensure that for any founders or staff that hold shares there is a 'bad leaver' clause that covers what happens to any shareholding on departure.

- Ensure that there is a good database / CRM that holds all contact details and is able to track interaction with customers, partners or any stakeholders.

- Ensure that all regulatory and similar requirements such as GDPR, insurance and the like are properly diarized and renewed on time.

- Have clear and consistent customer engagement routines and onboarding procedures if required.

It is also much easier to establish systems and procedures when a business is in its infancy and its operations are relatively simple. The later this decision is put off, and the larger and more complex a business grows, the more difficult, time consuming, and expensive it becomes to establish such procedures. Not only that, but in the meantime the business has been operating inefficiently and inevitably taking higher risks than it should have been.

Every good business needs good corporate governance, and whilst there are many different aspects to it, having good systems and procedures in place should certainly be seen as being one of the foundation stones. So, if your business is one of the many that do not have any such procedures already in place, the only questions that should be asked is what is needed and how soon can they be established? Conduct a gap analysis, or better still arrange an outsider to do this, that will highlight all the shortcomings and then arrange to rectify them as a matter of urgency.

22.

CASHFLOW MANAGEMENT

It is often said that turnover is vanity and profit is sanity. But, even more importantly, do not forget the reality that cash is king. Put simply, businesses fail because they do not have enough cash or other liquid assets to pay their bills or meet their immediate obligations. So, whilst increasing turnover and profitability are what every business owner is aiming to achieve, always remember to keep a strong focus on cashflow and the levels of cash in the business.

In some sectors and businesses this is easy. These are typically service businesses or those that do not need to keep large stocks, where sales are made on a cash with order or payment on delivery basis. In other sectors and businesses, however, managing cash can be much more of a challenge. These would be where the business needs to carry large or valuable stocks, or where the buyers expect to have time to pay for the goods purchased.

Another factor in the ease or otherwise of managing cash is where a business is in its growth cycle. Growing businesses consume cash as they constantly need to pay for all that goes with expansion, whilst mature businesses tend to have a more stable cash requirement which is easier to manage.Businesses that are scaling typically have to invest cash and have a higher burn rate covered by investment or debt, which demand close management. So remember the following points to keep sufficient cash in the business and steer clear of the implications of running short:

- **Capital**. Growing businesses consume cash and are particularly vulnerable to failure as they can simply run out of money. The younger a business is, the more difficult it is to borrow money. In turn, it means that any funding must be supplied by the founders or external investors. The point that many founders often do not appreciate is that raising external finance will normally take around six months, so a business should have a runway of around twelve months of cash at any time.

- **Stock**. Keep a close watch on stock levels, so you have enough to satisfy demand without having to finance too much and tie up cash. Also, it is imperative that these is no dead stock. Any stock that is dead should be discounted and sold in order to free up cash.

- **Purchases**. Wherever possible, it normally pays to take advantage of any deferred payment terms (ie, 30, 60 or 90 days) if these are available at no or low cost. However, as a smaller or new business these are often not available.

- **Sales**. The perfect situation is that your sales are on a 'payment with order' basis or at least on delivery, as not only is this good for cashflow, but it also protects against any possibility of bad debt. In an ideal situation you obtain deferred payment terms from your suppliers whilst at the same time achieving payment with order on your sales as this produces positive cashflow.

- **Margins**. Try to keep profit margins as healthy as possible, as not only will this, of course, produce the greatest profit, but it will also inject as much cash as possible into the business, enabling you to purchase more stock or cover other costs and scale faster.

- **Cash reserves**. As well as having a long enough runway of capital, your management of payment flows in and out matters just as much. One trap for many new businesses is not putting any VAT received on sales to one side so they don't have the cash to pay HMRC when it is due.

- **Costs**. Early-stage businesses will benefit by keeping as many of their costs as possible variable, rather than taking on too many fixed costs, as this allows for more flexibility and reducing some short-term costs in times of need.

A focus on these points will maximize your cashflow and make sure it is property managed. It will benefit how you manage the rest of your business as well. Once cash is recognized as king, mattering more than turnover and even profit in the short term, how is it best preserved?

You do not need to be an accountant to understand that the balance sheet details a company's assets and liabilities, the profit and loss account details income and expenditure and what is left at the end, and the cashflow statement summarizes the amount of cash and cash equivalents entering and leaving a company.

Banks use two different ratios when analysing a company's ability to meet its short-term financial obligations as a measure of its strength. The first, and more generally applied, is the liquidity ratio, which measures how much cash and other liquid assets that a business can easily turn into cash within a year and is available to pay short-term liabilities due within a year.

The second, and more stringent, is the acid test or quick ratio, which compares a company's most short-term assets to its most short-term liabilities to see if a company has enough cash to pay its immediate liabilities, such as bills and short-term debt. This ratio disregards current assets that might be difficult to liquidate quickly such as stock. It is worth mentioning these ratios as it highlights how importantly banks and other analysts view cashflow.

One last piece of explanation about two different types of cost that any business has. These are, of course, fixed and variable. Fixed costs are those costs such as rent, rates, salaries and loan repayments that must be made irrespective of whether you actually sell anything that week or month. Variable costs are those costs such as raw materials, energy consumption and other such direct inputs that are more directly linked to the production of your product. That is, if your business increases or decreases production then variable costs increase or decrease proportionally. Over a longer period, all fixed costs are variable when a company scales up or reduces the size of its operations, for example, when they move to larger offices or close a factory.

With this knowledge, it becomes more obvious how best to preserve cashflow in your business. Based on these principles for managing cashflow management, it is worth reviewing how these might work in practice for smaller businesses where the ideal position is not always achievable, so preserving cashflow typically comes down to utilizing as many of the following as you can:

- Obtain payment terms that are as long as possible and do not actually pay until necessary.

- Encourage buyers to pay you as soon as possible, even by offering some form of incentive.

- Try not to incur costs until you actually need to by adopting policies such as ordering raw materials as late as feasible, but don't forget to always allow for some delay as otherwise this can damage your business.

- Any business that is expanding is always cash hungry, so in really tough times cash can be preserved by not expanding in any way.

- Put off taking on any new staff until a later stage and not immediately replacing any staff that leave.

- Again, in lean times it is possible to reduce stocks or levels of production and this frees up cash.

Some of these last points should only be used *in extremis* as they can lead to the contraction of the business, at least in the short term, but there are times when it can be better to reduce the scale of your operation and survive rather than fail. When looking to expand, investment or some alternative form of finance will let you meet cashflow demands with sufficient margin to cover unforeseen circumstances.

23.

WHY IT'S HARD
TO SCALE

According to UK government statistics, some 660,000 new companies are established each year and many of these will have plans to scale rather than to remain a micro business. As with everything about starting a business, different people do it for different reasons, and they have different levels of ambition. Some people want it to remain a side hustle or a modest lifestyle business, whilst others have plans from day one to scale and grow into a multimillion-pound, international operation.

Given these variations, what scaling means to you will differ. It might involve taking on a single employee or it could mean expanding internationally and buying out a rival business.

Whatever the scale of your implementation, many of

the recommendations about how to best go about it are the same in principle. If, as a founder, your plans are to stay as a side hustle or a lifestyle business, then in many ways life is much simpler, as it is not necessary to take on all the additional responsibilities that scaling brings with it. Micro businesses often do not raise any external equity finance or even hire any senior staff, just to name two differences. However, in order to scale a business in a more meaningful way, you will face a series of challenges:

- **Time management**. Running any business, but especially a growing one, is likely to mean that there is always too much to do and too little time. So you have to work smart and manage all time as effectively as possible. Different people do this in different ways but finding something that works for you will greatly increase productivity.

- **Systems and procedures**. Large-scale businesses could not operate without having detailed and sophisticated systems and procedures in place. Whilst a smaller business is of course simpler to run, having good systems and procedures in place will, nevertheless, lead to a more streamlined and efficient operation and one that is less prone to make errors. Put systems in place from the outset as it is much easier and cheaper while still a small business rather than to wait and do it later.

- **Finance**. Any growing business consumes cash, as it is typical that there is a time lag between costs associated with scaling and any income earned as a larger operation. For many businesses, it means that there is a need to raise finance. Most founders underestimate the amount of time and effort it takes to raise finance and so often leave starting the process much later than is ideal. Make sure that you leave plenty of time and have a long enough cash runway for the business to survive in the meantime. Also make sure that whatever amount raised is sufficient for your plans in the foreseeable future. Remember that you may well need to raise further funding in the future and dilute your shareholding further.

- **Timing**. As well as getting the timing right for raising finance, it has to be right in the life of the business. Too soon and it will not be possible to raise the amount of finance required to achieve all that is wanted. Too late and the business will already have foregone some of the better growth opportunities. In some business sectors, it is imperative that the business scales rapidly in order to ensure that they stay ahead or, at least, keep up with the competition, whilst in other sectors scaling is more about taking existing market share and speed is less important.

- **Staffing**. As the business grows, then so too does the level of staffing. Not only is it necessary to ensure that the total number of staff grows in line with the size of the business but, even more essential is that the size and capability of the senior management team also stays ahead of all the other requirements of scaling. Senior hires are often rewarded with some form of share options as this helps ensure that you are able to attract the best recruits but on a limited budget.

- **Premises**. Depending on the activities of your business, it is almost inevitable that as the operation scales your business will need to take on more space, whether that is office, retail, manufacturing or storage. As with so many things, getting the timing right with this will impact on many other areas. If done too early, it consumes cash unnecessarily. If not done early enough, then it can restrict any growth opportunities. Considerations such as how far can you increase production, or even just sales, before having to make a step change such as moving offices or production and make further investment into fixed costs are major considerations.

- **Advisory board**. Any business, other than a micro business, with plans to grow, really should have a good advisory board to help guide and nurture the business

WHY IT'S HARD TO SCALE

as well as to help with contacts and assist in many other ways.

- **Human resources, legal and accounting**. As any business grows in size, it also grows in complexity and has greater needs. Just as a good advisory board will play a major role in the scaling journey, then so too can working with good external advisors when needed.

- **Marketing and public relations**. Increasing exposure in any way should lead to more enquires and ensure your funnel of sales leads is constantly being topped up. In order to scale it is necessary to focus more attention on this area as really successful businesses have mastered the art of converting a high number of leads into sales. It may be that this is done with incentives, superb customer experience and helping clients on every step of the sales journey. Or it may simply be by having the best offering at the best price and being able to demonstrate that in one way or another.

- **International growth**. If scaling your business internationally, then it brings a whole new range of challenges and care should be taken that everything is done to minimize risks and costs but whilst maximizing any opportunities.

Exactly what needs to be done and when will depend upon a multitude of factors. These will include what sector your business is in; whether it is pre-revenue, revenue, or making profit; what your growth ambitions are; how big your potential market is and whether it is just UK or international. In addition, the answer will also depend upon analysing at what stage your business is now and where the pinch points are in your supply chain or customer service delivery, and then taking action to strengthen those first.

Scaling also brings with it other considerations. For example, the higher your fixed costs, the higher your risks of a downturn in sales, so how much can you scale whilst not committing to fixed costs? So it is prudent to consider strategies, such as can you lease or hire rather than buy.

Not only are all of the above points relevant to all businesses looking to scale, whatever the size, but they also all share an element of the sooner the better. Like everything in business, doing the right things at the right time can make all the difference.

So many small businesses fail unnecessarily because the founder has refused to either delegate or listen to advice or, even more commonly, to sell any equity that will inject funds into the business that will allow the company to grow properly. The best and most forward-thinking founders are those that accept that they may not necessarily be the best person to make all the decisions once the company grows. Retaining a hundred percent of a small company, or worse still a failed one, is of course much less rewarding in every way than holding a smaller percentage in a larger, thriving business.

As the business grows, founders need to be able to delegate and to lead teams rather than doing everything themselves or exercising direct control. At this stage, the relevance of business culture will start to play an ever greater role. It can be difficult to keep the dynamics sound, if taking on many new staff at the same time and evolving from a small start-up to a more mature and larger company.

With some businesses, or in some sectors, scaling a business is critical. This is typically where barriers to entry are lower, and the threat of meaningful competition grows quickly. If you do not exploit the market opportunity then your competitor will. This can be especially true in the tech sector for example.

Somewhere along this growth path most businesses will plateau, at least for a time, whilst the next steps are worked out and then implemented. Having the foresight to know that the challenges change with each step of your business journey enables you to plan your strategy and finances accordingly. It will give you a much smoother ride and greatly increase your chances of success.

24.

HOW TO ADAPT
AND PIVOT

We live in changing times. Rapidly changing times. It is
no surprise that many founders, both first-time and serial
entrepreneurs, often ask themselves 'where do I go from
here?'. But change always brings opportunity, whether this
change is caused by environmental concerns, technological
change or a global pandemic does not alter that by
recognising those changed circumstances and by adapting
or pivoting your business accordingly it can be possible to
scale even more quickly.

Bill Gates, co-founder of Microsoft, said: 'we always
overestimate the change that will occur in the next two
years and underestimate the change that will occur in the
next ten. Don't let yourself be lulled into inaction'. As the
speed of change increases, it becomes ever more true. We

see it all around us in every field of both our personal and professional lives. Every business should always be looking to adapt by evolution, they should also be ready to pivot by revolution in need or if an opportunity presents itself.

The global coronavirus pandemic of 2020 that led to lockdowns across the world has forced many companies to adapt and pivot rapidly. This period has led many more founders than normal to question what are the next steps and, if everything is changing, what they must do in order to stay ahead of the curve? For businesses in the United Kingdom, Brexit has added even more uncertainty and the need for the majority of businesses to adapt how they work.

Technology has become the great definer. Whether this is fintech, edtech, healthtech or any other tech, the ever more rapid advances have created huge opportunities. And, as ever, it is the start-ups and early-stage businesses that are normally not only the quickest to spot them but also the ones that are most able to act on them and to respond in the shortest possible time.

Any business at any stage of its life must be able to adapt and change to changing circumstances. One of the real benefits that early-stage businesses have is that they are small and fast on their feet and are therefore perfectly structured to be able to react swiftly to changing circumstances. The larger the company and the more layers of management and complex reporting systems that they have, the slower most of them become in making decisions.

Events normally unfold at a slower pace than we have witnessed recently. Even so you always have to adapt and pivot more quickly than either the existing competition or any potential new challengers. This can be achieved in many ways but include the constant monitoring of your competitors and the wider marketplace, product and technological change, consumer demand and behaviour, and cultural and ethical changes. Essentially, it is understanding all the inputs that are present in a buyer's mind, whether consciously or subconsciously, before they decide whether to become your customer or go to a competitor.

It is, of course, impossible to predict the future, but it is most certainly possible to define trends or identify needs and wants that are not being met by goods or services that are presently available. Identifying such gaps are the first steps towards formulating the answer for how best to adapt your business and understand where to take it next and how to improve and scale it. Sometimes it can seem that change is happening for no apparent reason, but the driver is always to improve something in some way.

A survey conducted in spring 2020 by Be the Business, an industry-led productivity leadership group, from discussions with its network of 250,000 people and a survey of 500 small firms, and reported in the *Financial Times*, found that 21 percent had pivoted their business in a meaningful way. We can all think of many companies selling products that they did not before the lockdowns or providing services in a different way. Some obvious examples are eat-in restaurants that started offering a home delivery service or local bakeries selling home baking kits.

Some statistics suggest that as many as 40 percent of companies that have pivoted in a fundamental way have actually increased sales from pre-lockdown levels. For the remaining 60 percent of pivoters it has at least produced sufficient income to ensure their survival. These numbers show how significant this tactic has been for many thousands of companies. Many of those 40 percent that have increased sales are likely to focus their new post-lockdown model on the new business even when they have also re-introduced their original activities. For some, it will mean a total pivot into a new area and one where they may never have ventured without being forced to think creatively. For the remaining 60 percent, many will retain some aspects of their new revenue streams, so will have pivoted to a degree.

For all of them, speed of reaction matters. To gain most from pivoting, it has to happen as soon as feasible. Alternatively, it will let you stem your losses more quickly.

Whilst it may be harsh to say, quite a number of

businesses that have failed in recent years could have survived by pivoting rather than just trying to do exactly the same thing as they were before a change such as lockdown or by preserving their cash.

Given that change should always be embraced and not seen as a threat, how should businesses go about adapting and pivoting?

- **Timing**. As with everything in business, much depends on timing. Failing to adapt or pivot can be a quick way for your business going from doing well to struggling or even failing totally. However, adapting or pivoting too soon when the market is not ready for your new offering, or when the technology is not as widely accepted as necessary, can also lead to major problems. There are many examples of both, but there is no doubt that not reacting quickly enough is by far the most typical.

- **Adapting**. In many ways adapting can be seen as being something of a partial or gentle pivot. In business, the client is always right and what people or businesses want to buy evolves over time. This, if for no other reason, means that your business should constantly adapt to meet changing demand. Generally, this adaptation is incremental, but any good business owner should also always be looking to take advantage of changing circumstances by bringing in different but complementary offerings, thus opening up new markets whilst retaining the existing ones.

- **Pivoting**. On occasion, circumstances are such that simply adapting may not be enough. This may be caused by some form of uncontrollable outside event, such as a lockdown, totally disrupting your original business. Or it may be by choice, as new but radically different markets open up offering potentially better opportunities. Pivoting purely out of choice is much more courageous, but can have exactly the same consequences. History tells us that many of the more visionary businesspeople who pivot at the right moment are those who do best.

- **Never get complacent**. Just because you may offer the best product or service at the best price one month, does not mean that that will always be the case. Being at, or near, the top of the tree takes a lot of effort to get there and just as much effort to stay there. So constantly assess every aspect of your competitive environment.

- **Research and development**. Products and services evolve at a rapid pace. As soon as you have brought out a new or revised product, you should instantly be starting to look at the next version or new product.

- **Revolution, not just evolution**. Do not just take incremental steps but be prepared to take major leaps forward. Be more radical, so that you can properly disrupt the market.

- **Review your business model**. Even in normal times, you should constantly review your business model and ask if you are doing everything in the best and most efficient way possible. Are your costs well controlled and your supply chain secure? Are your systems and procedures as slick as possible?

- **Be brave**. To be an entrepreneur or a business owner takes a certain type of person, who is typically self-reliant and self-confident, as well as being brave and unafraid to act. Adapting your original business takes courage.

Whether time and circumstances move more sequentially or whether they race by more exponentially, it does not alter the need to constantly reassess everything that impacts on your business. With this constant flow of information, you are then able to make informed decisions about whether your business should simply evolve, adapt or pivot more radically.

25.

GROWTH CAPITAL

As your business has grown and started to raise some initial outside investment, the pre-seed and seed investment is most likely to have come from business angels or crowdfunding, or from a combination of the two. However, as the business continues to grow it is probable that it will not only need to raise further funding but also raise larger amounts. The most prominent providers of growth funding are venture capital firms. Ultimately, as the business continues to grow one of the ultimate ways of raising funding is an initial public offering (IPO) where the company's shares are listed on a recognized stock exchange. Traditional VCs would exit at this point or through other routes, such as sale to a strategic buyer.

A VC is a professional firm of investors. It will conduct detailed analysis and due diligence, often pushing much harder for a bigger percentage of the company, giving you a lower valuation. VCs are more typically seen in second or third round funding or for larger amounts, although some do specialize at the smaller end of the market but focus on high-growth tech companies. The funding process can become much longer and more painful for a smaller business due to the level of information required, but once a VC is on board the fact that they are professionals means that they can be a good business partner and will often look to invest in subsequent, larger rounds.

Funding rounds are classified by both sequence and amounts raised. The first small rounds are referred to as pre-seed and seed rounds, then progressing through rounds A, B, C, D etc. It is difficult to give precise details about what their parameters are, as these can change from one VC to another, but if a VC states that its focus is on B rounds and above, then they will not be interested in investing £500,000 in your first fundraising, so should not be approached if that is what you are looking for. Indeed, it is important to research the requirements of any VC before they are approached and details will be found on their websites.

Historically, VCs have focused on companies with more traction that are looking to raise £5m plus. However, in more recent times, there are a growing number of VCs that are interested in investing as little as £500,000 or even less, if they believe that the business will need further investment in the future. VCs will subject you and your business to much higher levels of due diligence than any other source and it is for this reason that they will normally take longer to conclude an investment. They tend to have a sector focus and expertise, as well as wanting to appoint a board director. Moreover, they will charge annual fees and will take more charges overall than most other sources of investment.

When seeking investment from a VC it would be normal to expect to have to put together a data room. This is simply a central place where all required information can be viewed. The data will include everything from your certificate of incorporation and articles of association, existing shareholder and any finance agreements, bank statements, employee and supplier contracts, any lease or rental agreements, and all other information that will enable them to fully assess the legal and financial position of the business. The data room would also include the full business plan and forecast financials, any previous annual or management accounts, and the pitch deck. Put simply, anything that a VC would need in order for them to complete detailed due diligence and to get a full understanding of your business's past performance and its future forecasts.

Increasingly, VCs are also more flexible in considering some form of structured financing package that will provide both equity and debt. They are able to do this as they will become significant minority shareholders and are able to take a view on their overall exposure and risk/reward profile, as well as looking at when the capital is repaid. The benefit to you as a founder is that you will need to sell less equity in your business. This structure may include converting debt into equity or equity into debt, depending upon how the business performs against forecast or pre-agreed performance indicators.

Many VCs have a preference for a clean capitalization table: that is, fewer shareholders owning larger stakes, as it is easier to communicate with shareholders to run the business. The cap table is the shareholder register which lists out by name each of the shareholders and how many shares that they hold in the business. Because of the way that many early-stage businesses go about raising finance, there are often a large amount of investors on the cap table that actually own a small percentage of the business. Depending on a number of circumstances this can put some VCs off investing in a business or they will only do so if the smaller shareholders agree to sell their stake.

It is worth noting that the major crowdfunding platforms use a nominee shareholding structure, which means that it is only the one investor, ie, the crowdfunding platform, that is on the cap table as they then hold the shares as nominee for all the beneficial owners of the underlying shares. Despite that, some VCs do not like seeing crowdfunding platforms on the cap table either, although they would favour nominee structures rather than many individual angel investors.

As such, whenever you look to raise finance for your growing business, it pays to consider all the ramifications of how much you raise, at what valuation, and where from, as some decisions in the earlier stages may limit your choices later in your growth. Clearly, the amount that you can raise is ultimately linked to the valuation of the business, as it will dictate what percentage needs to be sold in order to raise the new investment.

When new funding is raised, it is done by the company issuing new shares, so whilst the number of shares held by existing shareholders remains the same the percentage of the business that they own is diluted. Founders need to ensure that they do not dilute their holding too much, particularly in a higher growth business that expects to raise funding multiple times at ever increasing valuations. Each time, any existing shareholders are diluted. Founders with too small a shareholding in their own business can become disincentivised, which can undermine the business.

VCs are well aware of this problem and would normally look to raise a large minority stake, typically in the region of 25 percent. Another notable metric for VCs is exit from their investment in five years or a little more and make a tenfold gain. By using the forecast valuation of the business at the time of potential exit, they calculate what percentage of the business they would need to own now and at what valuation in order to achieve the desired exit multiple.

If your business is related to tech and based in London, then you have an added advantage of accessing VC funding, as London is Europe's global tech city. In 2020, London-based tech firms raised more than $10.5 billion in new investment from VCs, which they are expected to surpass in 2021. The reason that VCs like tech-based businesses is that they can often scale quickly and so provide good potential for high returns.

A survey released by Dealroom and London & Partners in early spring 2021 shows that not only has London been the second fastest-growing mature tech ecosystem in the world since 2016, but it is also the only European city in the global top ten for VC investment. Despite the pandemic, funds continued to be available for the right companies with the right stories. Currently, London stands fifth in the world rankings, only behind Beijing, San Francisco, New York and Shanghai.

Fintech remained the favoured sector for VC investment in London, representing 41 percent of funds deployed, equating to some $4.3bn. These figures do not include enterprise software or cybersecurity which represented a further 17 percent and 6 percent of funds invested. Healthtech and edutech are strong sectors too.

Whilst these statistics are impressive enough, and undoubtedly cover the vast majority of funds raised, remember that they are based only on funds invested by VC firms and so the total amount of funding will be higher. The amount of pre-seed, seed, and even series A funding, that goes into the fintech sector from crowdfunding, high-net-worth individuals, family offices and the like, not only adds to the amount of funds invested, but it is also a necessary component in ensuring that tech companies are able to raise the initial funds to grow sufficiently to then be able to attract funding from VCs in the future.

APPENDIX 1

TAX RELIEF FOR INVESTORS: SEIS AND EIS

In a book dealing with business from start-up to scale-up with a particular focus on funding such growth, it is impossible not to mention the tax benefits provided by the United Kingdom's government to those investing in early-stage businesses. These are two closely related schemes that are known as SEIS and EIS: or the Seed Enterprise Investment Scheme and the Enterprise Investment Scheme.

They were created to encourage investment from UK tax-domiciled individuals into UK registered start-ups and early-stage businesses. Essentially, both operate in the same way. Although SEIS is more advantageous, it has greater restrictions than EIS.

Many private investors that invest in early-stage businesses, whether it is as a business angel, via a crowdfunding platform or any other route, do so because of the advantages offered to them through these two schemes. If your business is not approved and registered for such schemes then raising pre-seed and seed investment from private individuals will be so much more difficult.

The majority of UK-registered early-stage businesses qualify, although there are some restrictions on sectors or activities, such as farming or running a hotel. The business must also be under a certain age and size, and with a limited number of employees. It is the business that applies to HMRC, the UK tax authority, for 'advanced assurance' that when they start to raise funding that investment into the business will qualify. As the tax relief is claimed by the individual investor, it depends on the individuals' own personal circumstances as to whether they will actually receive the tax benefits. In order to qualify the investor mut pay tax in the UK and the scheme is not open to founders, although they can claim tax relief in other ways. It is also not available to individuals who are parents or children of the founders, although it is available to siblings.

What exactly is the difference between SEIS and EIS?

SEIS

- Company maximum inward investment eligible: £150,000.

- Period from first commercial sale to investment: a maximum of two years.

- Company maximum gross assets when shares issued: £200,000.

- Maximum number of staff: 25

- Tax relief on investment for the investor: can claim 50 percent of investment made.

- Tax relief for the investor on any losses made: yes, at highest rate tax paid for net investment.

EIS

- Company maximum inward investment eligible: £12 million.

- Period from first commercial sale to investment: a maximum of seven years.

- Company maximum gross assets when shares issued: £15 million.

- Maximum number of staff: 250.

- Tax relief on investment for the investor: can claim 30 percent of investment made

- Tax relief for the investor on any losses made: yes, at highest rate tax paid for net investment

Under both schemes all income and capital gains are exempt from tax, as well as any shareholding being exempt from inheritance tax.

As can be imagined, there are many intricate details to these schemes. Any business owner or investor should familiarise themselves with them before going further. A full rundown can be found on the HMRC website.

This brief summary highlights the benefits to investors and why the schemes play such an integral role in raising finance. Under both, individuals gain tax refunds on investments made, as well as on any losses. As such, the schemes significantly reduce both the initial net amount invested, as well as the risks, thus making any investment much more attractive.

APPENDIX 2
R & D TAX CREDITS

R&D stands for research and development and the R&D tax credit scheme can be a great financial incentive for any business to undertake more R&D. According to the official report from HMRC, the United Kingdom's tax authority: 'R&D tax credits are a tax relief designed to encourage greater R&D spending, leading in turn to greater investment in innovation. They work by either reducing a company's liability to corporation tax or by making a payment to the company'.

There are a number of notable points about this valuable giveaway to companies. The first is that whilst it is estimated that some 750,000 companies would be eligible to claim some form of tax refund under this scheme, in the tax year 2018/19 (the last full year for which complete figures are available), only 59,265 companies actually claimed under it and only 52,160 of them were small or medium-sized enterprises. Whilst the scheme is becoming more widely known as more specialists are established to help with claims, it remains relatively unknown. It seems that many accountants either do not know about it or for one reason or another do not advise their clients about it.

Companies can of course make the claims themselves, but there are now many specialist firms or accountants that offer the service based purely on a success fee. Most of them argue that their knowledge of the system and what can actually be claimed enables them to obtain a higher refund overall, as well of course as doing all of the work. They would also be best placed to see if any back claims would be possible. Fees typically range from between 5 percent to 25 percent of a successful claim. Those charging the higher fees maintain they offer a more bespoke service and an ability to obtain higher claims.

The point about what can actually be claimed for is an extremely valid one as the vast majority of companies believe that a company must be doing some form of technical R&D and can only claim limited costs. The reality is actually almost the opposite. Exactly what percentage of what claimable cost varies, but essentially it covers the majority of costs associated with a qualifying project, including: consumables; energy; staff costs (both specialists working full time on the project and any senior managers and others working part time, including sub-contractors); and most other direct and indirect costs.

As to the project itself, again many companies would say that they were not inventing anything, so would discount the possibility of R&D tax credits, but the scheme applies as much to adaptation and innovation as it does to invention. Most companies are looking to adapt what is already available, which can be everything from systems for customer relationship management to saving energy. Start-ups in particular are often trying to challenge or disrupt existing markets.

Perhaps the best bit of advice would be that if you start to do a project that you think even might qualify then it is best to do project accounting for it: that is, record all the costs separately as that will be the easiest way to prove the costs and maximize the claim.

Most later stage companies make R&D tax credit claims by way of tax relief on tax due, but what is attractive for start-ups and early-stage businesses is that even if the company is loss-making, the claim can be paid by bank transfer from HMRC, albeit at a slightly lower rate. Payments made to the company are normally received swiftly. Another beneficial feature of the scheme is that for those companies not having made a claim previously, then claims can be made going back two years and not just for the present year.

It is worth considering all that your business has done over the last two years that might enable you to claim an R&D tax credit, then speak to a few companies that could advise you on that or make the claim on your behalf. These cash injections can be the lifeblood that keeps an early-stage business going as they are often tight on cash.

ACKNOWLEDGEMENTS

A number of people have asked me how long the book has taken me to write. In many ways the answer is 40 years, as it is based on my experiences and knowledge built up over that time. It would be truer to say that it has been my mentoring experience and the establishment of Boom & Partners in more recent years that was the real catalyst. Putting pen to paper was the easy part.

None of this would have been possible without working with many fantastic entrepreneurs and founders, both those I have mentored and those who are clients. It is their drive, enthusiasm and innovative thinking that inspires me to want to help them on their journey from start-up to scale-up. I would also like to thank the other great business partners with who I have worked in recent years to help as many early-stage businesses as possible.